OTR
Publications
Presents

The Toy Fox Terrier

Eliza L. Hopkins & Cathy J. Flamholtz

Eliza L. Hopkins
National, Aug. 15, 1998

TITLE PAGE: A holiday basket filled with Toy Fox Terrier puppies. These little charmers are "PR" McConnell's Dixie, Dancer and Daisy. They were bred by Diane McConnell, of Clovis, New Mexico.

THE TOY FOX TERRIER

ISBN 0-940269-01-5

©1988 by OTR Publications

Printed in the United States of America

10 9 8 7 6 5 4 3 2

OTR PUBLICATIONS
P.O. Box 1243
Ft. Payne, Alabama 35967

Dedication

To Phil Hopkins and his interest in owning, producing, promoting and supporting top quality Toy Fox Terriers

Contents

Preface

I distinctly remember the first time I heard of the Toy Fox Terrier. While tales of the dog's devotion to man fill the pages of canine literature, this turn-about story has remained with me since childhood. It seems that there was a little boy in a southern city. His devoted companion was a Toy Fox Terrier. The two were inseparable, sharing their days in the reckless abandon found only in childhood. The lad's family had recently moved to a small apartment. The cramped quarters annoyed the boy's mother and one day she made a fateful announcement...the dog must go! She'd expected a tearful scene, with pleas to let the dog stay. Instead, the boy and his dog disappeared.

Soon, a clamor drifted up to the apartment window. Looking out, Mom saw her son marching resolutely on the sidewalk. He held a large sign. "I'm on strike. My Mother is unfair," it proclaimed. "She wants to throw out my dog." Matching him, stride for stride, was the little Toy Fox Terrier. A diminutive sandwich board astride her back read, "I don't want to go."

The Mother was undoubtedly amused, but expected the episode to fade quickly. Little boys, after all, aren't known for their patience. But the pair maintained their vigil. They had a mission. By afternoon, they'd attracted quite a crowd. Photographers and journalists, eager for a human interest story, interviewed the duo. Neighborhood children joined the march. Cars stopped, touched by the plight of a boy and his love for his dog.

In the meantime, Mom was beginning to soften. It seemed ridiculous to her that this much fuss would be made over a dog. It was, however, apparent that her son was determined. Finally, she was presented with a petition, bearing close to fifty signatures. Above the names was a simple, yet poignant plea: "Please let the boy keep his dog!" Mom relented and the Toy Fox Terrier stayed with his creative, pint-sized owner.

Over the years, I met a few Toy Fox Terriers. I discovered that this breed engendered tremendous devotion from owners. They would have understood that little boy's intense loyalty to his dog. I suppose, when researching the Toy Fox Terrier chapter for my previous book, *A Celebration of Rare Breeds,* I'd hoped to find someone with the awe-inspiring devotion of that young boy. I did, indeed, find that someone in Eliza Hopkins. She generously and patiently fielded all my questions about the breed. Despite her busy schedule, she always found the time to help me. I couldn't have asked for a better source, for Eliza had that wonderful combination of long experience with the breed and unerring dedication to its future. What impressed me most, however, was her unstinting enthusiasm for Toy Fox Terriers. It was from this contact that the idea of writing a book on the Toy Fox Terrier was born.

Eliza and her late husband, Phil, obtained their first Toy Fox Terrier in the late 1950s. In the next few years, several litters were born on the Hopkins homestead. The real start of the well-known Hopkins Toy Fox Terrier Kennel, however, began in 1960. That year, the couple joined the Michigan Toy Fox Terrier Association and attended their first show. To this day, Eliza regards showing dogs as the greatest of hobbies. While she is now a U.K.C. licensed judge of the breed, her first love remains exhibiting her own dogs.

To date, sixty champions have come from the Hopkins Kennel, including thirteen Grand Champions. Five National Grand Champions have made their home at Eliza's kennel and another Hopkins bred dog attained this honor. Dogs from the Hopkins' Kennel have done much for the breed. National Grand Champion "PR" Yancey's Rinebold Skipper sired thirteen champions, including four Grand Champions and a National Grand Champion. The homebred, National Grand Champion "PR" Hopkins' Royal Inky, sired thirteen champions, including two Grand Champions. Dogs from Eliza's breedings have formed the foundation stock for many U.S. kennels. In addition, Toy Fox Terriers from Eliza's breedings have been sold to Canada, England and Japan.

Clearly, Eliza Hopkins could retire today and rest on her laurels. Instead, her commitment to the Toy Fox Terrier continues. One always feels that, with Eliza, the best is yet to come. After more than thirty years, her devotion to the breed still shines brightly. There is always the search for a better Toy Fox Terrier, built on the breed's greats. There's always another litter to be bred or another dog to be shown. This book is simply one more step in a lifetime spent promoting the breed and educating the public about the Toy Fox Terrier.

It is our great pleasure to present you with this book on the Toy Fox Terrier. While the words in the book are mine, they are born out of Eliza's extensive experience. It is our hope that this book will prove a source of information, previously unavailable, to the thousands of Toy Fox Terrier owners.

This book is meant as a tribute to all Toy Fox Terrier breeders, past, present and future. Our special gratitude goes to those who helped by contributing photos. Our special appreciation goes to the United Kennel Club, Inc., and Mr. Fred Miller, its President, who supplied us with needed information and granted us permission to reproduce the drawings which accompany the chapter on the Standard. Lastly, and most importantly, this book is a tribute to all Toy Fox Terriers. Perhaps we will be able to repay, in some small measure, their devotion to us.

Cathy J. Flamholtz
May, 1988

1

TFT History

The Toy Fox Terrier of today is an all-American breed. His roots, however, lie across the sea in merry old England. It has been a long genesis from the unkempt, scruffy dogs that were first labeled terriers to the handsome, sleek toy dogs seen in today's show rings. In the beginning, terriers were the working companions of British farmers. They aided rural homesteaders in ridding their lands of unwanted vermin. Later, when the small dogs became an integral part of the sport of foxhunting, the Smooth Fox Terrier was born. When styles in foxhunting changed, the little terrier seemed doomed. He was saved by the era of dog shows and kennel clubs. Within a few short years, he had soared to the top of British show circles. Americans grew to appreciate the Smooth Fox Terrier, too. He became a fixture in American show rings and one of the most popular breeds in the country. The TFT has been called the "little brother of the Smooth Fox Terrier." That he is, and he still retains the qualities that propelled the Fox Terrier to prominence.

EARLY TERRIERS (1500's–1700's)

We do not know how long terriers have existed in Great Britain. We do know that they date back as far as Julius Caesar's day. Scribes reported that there were "small dogs that would follow their quarry to ground." The 15th century book, *Field Sports,* contained a mention of these dogs. The terrier was described by Dr. Caius, personal physician to Queen Elizabeth, in the first dog book, written in 1557. He was primarily responsible for the appellation "terrier," which comes from the Latin *terra,* meaning "earth."

By the 1600's, England's kings were hunting with terriers. In a letter dated August 15, 1617, King James I asked a friend to secure terriers for the royal kennels. He requested the Laird of Caldwell "to search out and send to us two couples of excellent terriers or earth dogs, which are both stout fox killers and will stay in the ground."

In speaking of those early terriers, one of America's first Fox Terrier breeders, August Belmont, said, "The characteristics of the Terrier...were...a natural inclination to hunt and destroy vermin of any kind, pursuing it to its refuge wherever it be within the Terrier's power to reach it; this trait being accompanied by a sprightly and tense nature, keen sense of hearing, quick vision, a most unerring nose, and an indomitable gameness.

"Being intended to hunt with his master, he should be ready and eager to attack the object of the hunt, enter into its hiding place and indicating the locality by giving tongue or drawing out the game in the open....This style of hunting and fighting requires great dash, courage and dexterity."

FOXHUNTING AND THE BIRTH OF THE FOX TERRIER
(late 1700's–mid 1800's)

Originally, fox hunting was necessary, since this cunning critter was a formidable predator of small livestock. By the 1800's, foxhunting came to be regarded as a gentleman's sport. Sportsmen had discovered that chasing the fleet fox, through woods and across meadows, provided an ideal day's entertainment. Foxhounds, excelling in tracking ability and endowed with melodious voices, were developed specifically for use in the hunt. The sly fox was not to be outdone. To avoid capture, he would dart into a hole. Here he would snuggle safe and secure, while the frustrated hunters and their hounds milled above ground. Such resourcefulness put a prompt end to the day's sport.

Enter the terrier. It was discovered that the vermin dogs, so common on British farms, fit easily into foxholes. With their keen noses and abundant courage, they could cause the fox to bolt. The hounds and hunters could then, once again, take up the chase. Certainly, many a terrier saved the day's sport for the hunters. It was important that the terrier refrain from killing the fox, for this would have put a quick end to the day's outing. His purpose was to cause the fox to flee or, barring that, to pinpoint its location underground by barking. The hunters could then come to the dog's aid, and dig the terrier and his quarry from the hole. The little dogs became an important adjunct to the sport. "No foxhound establishment was considered complete without a brace of well-bred terriers," wrote Bewick in his 1790 book, *History of Quadrapeds.*

Foxhound kennels often employed a "terrier man," whose sole purpose was to attend to the terriers. He made sure that the dogs were on the spot when needed. In smaller establishments, the head groom sometimes served this purpose. While long legged terriers, capable of keeping up with the hounds, were sometimes employed, small terriers were often used. They were carried in leather bags, suspended from the saddle or slung across the terrier man's shoulder. Because of this practice, small terriers were often dubbed "the groom's pocket piece."

These early Fox Terriers varied greatly in type. The foxhunters cared not what the dog looked like, so long as he could perform afield. But, like all sportsmen, foxhunters were a competitive lot. Many an evening was spent recapping past hunting adventures, and word of a particularly adept dog spread quickly. A premium was paid for the puppies of a proficient hunter and he would be in demand as a stud. Selective breeding, based on performance, was widely practiced. Writing in the 1800's, John Walker described his visit to a Fox Terrier kennel. The proprietor, then eighty years of age, had been developing his strain of Fox Terriers for the past forty years. "Pedigree and blood have been held subservient to unflinching courage; for wherever the slightest indisposition was manifested to go at anything when told to do so, that specific animal was not permitted to perpetuate his or her species, and its canine form did not long annoy the eye of the owner nor disgrace his kennel."

To the best of our knowledge, the first Fox Terriers carried the blood of England's old Black and Tan Terrier. As the competitive fever to breed the best terriers escalated, hunters tried a variety of crossbreedings. Greyhound, Beagle and Bull Terrier blood was introduced. The Bull Terrier cross was, by far, the most controversial. Many owners decried this cross, for they felt that it gave the dog too much "fight" and caused him to engage the fox in combat, rather than flushing it.

The first National Grand Champion, the great "PR" Rinebold's Winkie, owned by Violet and Carl Rinebold.

Early Fox Terriers came in a wide variety of colors. In 1790, Bewick describes the myriad of colors available to the hunter. "Terriers of the best blood...are now, by the prevalence of fashion, bred of all colours, red, black (with tanned faces, flanks, feet and legs) and brindle-sandy; some few brown-pied, white-pied, and pure white." A new age was dawning, however. Fashion dictated that a good Fox Terrier was to be predominately white in color. We are told that this attribute had a practical purpose. It was said that the hounds, on occasion, mistook the terrier for the fox and promptly tore it asunder. Bewick suggests, however, that it was the young sportsmen who had trouble discerning the difference between the fox and the dog. Nevertheless, white color quickly won favor and became the hallmark of a good Fox Terrier.

The appropriate size for a Fox Terrier has always been a hotly debated topic. In general, most Fox Terriers fell within the 10-20 pound range, as a dog larger than this was considered too big to go to ground effectively. We do know that smaller Fox Terriers coexisted with their larger brethren. In 1867, the prominent writer Stonehenge reported, the "dog may weigh from 6 lb. to 10 lb., or even 20 lb.; but provided he is large enough for his calling, he cannot be too small. It is an advantage to keep down the size of certain dogs as much as possible, and to consider that two small terriers will do more than double the work of one large dog, whilst they consume no more..."

After the 1830's, the sport of foxhunting changed radically. Many of Britain's forests were cleared and, with more open land, foxhunting became a faster sport. The fox was easier to locate on the deforested land. More men signed on with hunt clubs and mounted their horses for the thrilling chase. Capturing a fox became a secondary consideration, for the real fun was riding at breakneck speed across the newly formed meadows. If a fox went to ground, the hunters might inquire if there was a terrier at the nearest farmstead. If a dog could not be found, it was back on the horses and off again. "Modern hunting, quick gallops and the go-aheadedness of the times have done away with the Fox

Terrier's occupation," lamented the dog writer, Rawdon Lee. By 1840, Blaine commented sadly, "the occupation of the Fox Terrier is almost gone."

While no longer fundamental to foxhunting, the Fox Terrier was still admired on British farms. As in days of old, he maintained a position of prominence as a vermin dog *par excellence*. Idstone, author of the early work *The Dog*, was an outspoken advocate of the Fox Terrier's work in this capacity. "Every fox-terrier ought to be a good vermin killer," he said in an 1860 letter to the British publication, *The Field*. "Only about one man in five hundred wants a terrier to run with hounds; but he wants a vermin dog, and if the dog does run with hounds, he must be a 'rat-trap' all the same. I admire beauty much, but I have a far greater respect for character and quality, and I prefer a rough diamond to a polished pebble."

THE RAPID RISE OF THE SMOOTH FOX TERRIER
(1860's–early 1900's)

With the decline in foxhunting, the Fox Terrier's future was in peril. It's true the breed could still be seen on farms, but the serious selective breeding had long been dominated by foxhunters. Fortunately for the breed, the dog show movement was dawning. Propelled along with this heady new avocation was the little foxhunting terrier. The rise of the Smooth Fox Terrier had officially begun. During those early days, there was no official standard. Therefore, the dogs which graced British show rings were of widely varying types. Indeed, almost any dog of primarily white color, with black and tan markings and a docked tail, was entered as a Fox Terrier. Very quickly, however, the establishments which had long bred terriers to accompany foxhound packs, established themselves as the ones to beat in the show ring. The kennels of Oakley, Quorn, Belvoir and Grove set the standards for excellence in the breed.

The first separate classes for Smooth Fox Terriers were offered in 1863. The breed took the fledgling show world by storm. There was a dramatic rise in support. In 1864, forty Fox Terriers appeared at the Nottingham show. By 1867 and 1868, the entries rose to 62. Several years later at Nottingham, the Smooth Fox Terrier entry was an astounding 270!

It's unlikely that the dog world of that time had seen anything like the boom of the Smooth Fox Terrier. He was immediately embraced by dog show fanciers. Soon he was a popular subject of prominent artists. While little attention had previously been paid to his pedigree, it was now proudly recorded in the newly established stud books of England's Kennel Club. An incredible demand sprang up for Smooth Fox Terrier puppies and breeding stock, and fantastic sums were paid for winning dogs. A club was formed to foster the breed and a magazine devoted exclusively to the Fox Terrier was established.

THE TOY TERRIERS

By the late 1800's, the dog show era was firmly underway. Another movement was afoot in England, too. The late 1800's became "the heyday of

Toy Dogdom." Fashionable women, and an occasional gentleman, took pride in being seen with a toy dog in their arms. As we've seen, small Smooth Fox Terriers had existed in England. Even in the very earliest dog shows, small Fox Terriers made a showing. One writer of the time, in discussing the diversity of size in Smooth Fox Terriers, tells us that some shows had "classes of small dogs deserving rather to be placed in a class for toys."

Stonehenge, in the 1887 edition of *The Dog in Health and Disease,* devotes a section to toy terriers. He describes the "black-tan, smooth," now known as the Toy Manchester, and the Yorkshire Terrier. Interestingly, he also mentions a toy version of the "fox terrier, which last are now frequently made such by young ladies of the present day. All these breeds, when toys, have the same points as their larger brethren, and differ only in weight, which should not exceed 5 or 6 lbs. at most."

So, we find that a Toy Fox Terrier actually existed in Great Britain in the 1800's. Why this toy version did not survive will forever remain a mystery. Certainly, one would have thought that, with the booming popularity of the Smooth Fox Terrier, this diminutive brother would have been an instant success. Instead, the ultimate creation of a Toy Fox Terrier would be left to enterprising American fanciers.

This important photo from the 1920's gives clues to the TFT's origin. These small Fox Terriers, who matured at 10-12 pounds, were owned by Lester Schuyler, father of current TFT fancier, Sky Hughes. The puppies are shown with fresh deer antlers. It was from small Fox Terriers, such as these, that the TFT was developed.

THE FOX TERRIER IN AMERICA

The first Fox Terriers arrived in this country in the late 1800's or early 1900's. They were an immediate success. Show fanciers discovered that the natty Smooth Fox Terrier was a formidable competitor in show rings. Farmers joined the British homesteader in admiring their vermin catching qualities. Youngsters begged their parents for a Smooth Fox Terrier, and the breed became an esteemed child's companion. The breed became so popular that the RCA Victor Company chose the Smooth to grace its logo, "His Master's Voice."

"Runts" from Smooth Fox Terrier litters became popular. They gained a reputation as the scrappiest and boldest of the lot. They were often called "Fyce" or "Fiest" dogs, testament to their feisty natures. Though small in size, owners found a multitude of uses for these mighty mites. They performed the traditional ratting functions, and joined the farmer in hunting squirrels and rabbits. Sometimes, they were even allowed to accompany the larger Coonhounds on night hunts.

The late Howard Currens, one of our prominent TFT breeders, remembered these dogs from his childhood. With great fondness he recalled a rat hunt, staged one Sunday. "The handlers would poke the rats from under the old log houses and the little dogs would catch them. When the day ended the dogs had accounted for 74 rodents."

Valued for their superior intelligence, these diminutive Fox Terriers sometimes served as canine entertainers. In the early days of this century, there was little entertainment for rural dwellers. Small circuses, sometimes called Dog and Pony shows, toured regionally. Very often, the dog chosen was the little Fox Terrier. He amazed audiences with his antics and gained a reputation for charm, agility and verve.

THE HARD ROAD TO RECOGNITION

The United Kennel Club began registering the Smooth Fox Terrier in 1912. Early Toy Fox Terriers, despite their small size, were registered, with the U.K.C., as Smooth Fox Terriers. However, in the mid-1920's, fanciers approached the U.K.C., seeking a separate and distinct category for their toy dogs. It took many years before they achieved their objective. Writing in 1961, Dr. E. G. Fuhrman, an early supporter of the TFT, recalled, "The breed did not

come about overnight as many seem to think, but through the efforts of many years, hard ones..." On February 24, 1936, official recognition was granted under the name Toy Fox Terrier. The first litter, composed of a single pup, was registered on February 24, 1936, by Mrs. I. H. Young, of Punxsutawney, Pennsylvania. On February 28, 1936, Mrs. E. T. Rosengrant, of Crichton, Alabama, registered a litter of two. "Finally the Toy was definitely established," Dr. Fuhrman recalls. "The hardest part was over with and now there was enough breeding stock to assure a continuation of the Toy Fox Terrier."

A photo from the 1950's. This five pound male is Riley's Little Jody, owned by Mr. & Mrs. Arvin Riley, of Crooksville, Ohio.

Today, the Toy Fox Terrier breeds so true to type that it's difficult for us to imagine the difficulties and hardships faced by those early breed pioneers. In those formative years, size was a grave concern in TFT circles. An article in a 1959 issue of *Bloodlines* said, "One of the constant battles is to keep the Toy Fox Terrier a true Toy breed of dog. We have those that want a larger type...any great variation in weight and size can be accomplished in a short period of time towards the Standard Size Fox Terrier....to go to the small size takes years..."

Those dedicated to the true Toy Fox Terrier, however, valiantly fought all attempts to make the TFT into a larger breed. Fortunately, they had the wholehearted support of the United Kennel Club. Dr. Fuhrman said, "Along the way there were a few who tried by nearly every means...to change the breed, to destroy it...and breed for bigger dogs than the Toy Standard called for. The real breeders fought this movement tooth and nail and along with *Bloodlines Journal* and the United Kennel Club won each battle for the survival of the Toy Fox Terrier breed."

Another problem plagued those early breeders. It had been firmly established that the Toy Fox Terrier would indeed remain a toy. This took concerted efforts on the part of breeders, for they had to eliminate oversize dogs from their breeding programs. Some breeders, however, sought a short cut. They introduced Toy Manchester and, most particularly, Chihuahua blood into their breeding programs, in order to quickly reduce size. Dedicated breeders were appalled and vigorously fought this effort to modify the breed. Once again, they had the strong backing of the United Kennel Club.

Writing in *Bloodlines,* Violet Rinebold, one of our early breeders, and owner of the first National Grand Champion "PR" Rinebold's Winkie, said, "Some crossed the TFT with the Chihuahua or Black and Tan Terrier. Those crossed with the Chihuahua were easy to pick out since they had bowed front legs, more of an apple head...and the tail set was too low."

Dr. E. G. Fuhrman was quite outspoken in denouncing this practice. In 1959, he warned, "The Toy Fox Terrier Associations...the National Association and the U.K.C. Registration Office are combining their efforts to keep the Toy Fox Terrier bloodline pure. We are watching for the injection of blood of any other breed in the Toy Fox Terrier..., particularly Chihuahua blood. ...It is time that this type of breeding was immediately stopped..."

With the continued commitment of dedicated breeders and the strong support of the United Kennel Club, those who sought to cross the Toy Fox Terrier with other breeds were defeated. On August 31, 1960, the United Kennel Club officially closed the stud file on the Toy Fox Terrier. Those days are, thankfully, far behind us. We all owe a debt of gratitude to those hardworking breed pioneers. Thanks to them, today's TFT bloodlines are pure.

FORMATION OF THE NATIONAL AND STATE CLUBS

A dramatic step toward breed progress was taken in the 1940's. Dr. E.G. Fuhrman proposed the formation of a club devoted specifically to the breed. His idea met with an enthusiastic response and, on August 13, 1949, a small band of fanciers assembled at the Hotel Phoenix, in Findlay, Ohio, to discuss the proposal. Dr. Fuhrman came prepared with a sample constitution and by-laws. With the adoption of these documents, the National Toy Fox Terrier Association was officially born. The early breeders attending this first meeting were: Mr. & Mrs. W.W. Bird, Findlay, OH; Mr. & Mrs. John F. Buchman, Tiffin, OH; Mr. & Mrs. Charles L. Dosher, Carmi, IL; Mr. & Mrs. Frank Jones, Aurora, IL.; Mr. & Mrs. F.J. Kempher, Van Buren, OH.; Mr. & Mrs. A.C. Lanich, Greenville,

The Influence of Pedigree...
The Rinebold Winkie Line

Nat. Gr. Ch. "PR" Rinebold's Winkie, owned by Rinebold Kennels.

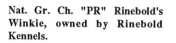

his daughter, "PR" Reed's Tiny Ann, also owned by Rinebold Kennels.

her son, "PR" Rinebold's Sir Captain, owned by Hopkins Kennel.

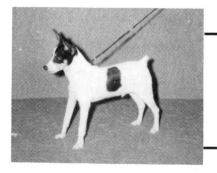

his daughter, Gr. Ch. "PR" Rinebold's Wee Judy, owned by Rinebold Kennels.

her son, Ch. "PR" Rinebold's Laddie Boy, owned by Rinebold Kennels. (Harkins photo)

his son, Nat. Gr. Ch. "PR" Yancey's Rinebold Skipper, owned by the Yanceys and purchased by Hopkins Kennel.

his son, Ch. "PR" Hopkins' Mr. Frosty, owned by Hopkins Kennel.

his son, Ch. "PR" Hopkins' Frosty Ace, owned by Hopkins Kennel.

his son, Gr. Ch. "PR" Singleton's Stormy Ace, owned by Jeri Singleton.

his son, Ch. "PR" Singleton's Mikimoto Ace, owned by Jeri Singleton.

11

OH.; Mr. & Mrs. Russell E. Mills, New Madison, OH; Mr. & Mrs. Carl V. Rinebold, Fostoria, OH; Mr. & Mrs. Neil Strole, Terre Haute, IN; and Mr. & Mrs. Robert Williams, Leipsic, OH.

Though this group was small, they were all committed to the breed and their enthusiasm was great. The following officers were elected to serve for 1949-1950. President: Mr. John F. Buchman; Vice President: Mr. Charles L. Dosher; Secretary/Treasurer: Mr. Neil Strole; and Publicity Director: Mr. Frank Jones. The following members agreed to serve as Directors: Mr. W. W. Bird; Dr. E. G. Fuhrman; Mrs. Bessie Kempher; Mrs. Violet E. Rinebold and Mr. Robert Williams.

The first official show of the National Toy Fox Terrier Association was held on August 19, 1950, in Tiffin, Ohio. The members selected Mr.

Ch. "PR" Corlett's Babbie Lady, owned by George and Sky Hughes, was California's first champion TFT.

Herman F. Boes, an experienced TFT breeder, to officiate. He became the very first licensed TFT judge. The show was rather simple by today's standards. Entry fees were $1.00 for the first entry and fifty cents for each additional entry by the same owner. Carl and Violet Rinebold donated a trophy for the Best of Show and Dr. E. G. Fuhrman contributed two engraved silver trays to be awarded to the Best Male and Best Female of Show. Ribbons were presented to the other class winners. This show was a learning experience for all involved. Most had never been in a show ring before and had to learn what was expected. Many people attended merely to observe.

The stage had been set and subsequent shows would draw larger entries. The establishment of the National Club did much to spur interest in the breed. It also helped to educate owners in proper breed type. By 1952, there was sufficient interest for the formation of individual state clubs for the breed. The Ohio and Illinois organizations led the way. Since that time, the state clubs have grown steadily in membership. In addition, the establishment of the state clubs allowed enthusiasts more opportunities to show their dogs.

The Toy Fox Terrier has come a long way since those early days. In 1961, Dr. Fuhrman predicted, "There are many good things ahead for the Toy Fox Terrier breed and breeders and owners of these fine little dogs." We have made dramatic progress and see many excellent dogs in the show ring today. With continued effort on the part of all breeders and owners, the Toy Fox Terrier will remain one of the most distinctive and desirable of the toy breeds.

2

TFT Character

The Toy Fox Terrier is a big dog in a little package. Though tiny, in comparison to other breeds, the TFT has the heart of a lion. The late dog writer and judge, Vincent Perry, once wrote that toy dogs "can have the courage of a Marine and the spirit of a tiger." Toy Fox Terrier breeders would certainly concur. The TFT is a combination of two great groups of dogs...the terriers and the toys. As such, he shares characteristics with both groups. Both have influenced his personality and character, and both of these components should be understood and appreciated by those who wish to own a TFT. Early breeders wished to capture the attributes of the Smooth Fox Terrier and condense them into a miniature version. They were eminently successful. The Toy Fox Terrier displays the keen intelligence, courage and animation that is the hallmark of all terriers. These are combined with the quintessential feature of all toy breeds...small size, devotion and an endless, abiding love for their masters.

The Toy Fox Terrier is a versatile little dog. Indeed, it's this versatility that enables the breed to be appreciated, on so many levels by such a variety of people. The TFT's small size makes him an ideal choice for people living in apartments, mobile homes or congested cities. Since he doesn't eat much, the TFT is an economical pet for senior citizens or families on limited budgets. With his terrier qualities, the TFT is also well suited to country locales. Many a TFT owner has discovered that his little dog is quite adept at catching mice and rats. Sportsmen have found that the Toy Fox Terrier makes a darn good squirrel dog, and some have even employed the little wonders on larger game. TFTs have a particularly acute sense of hearing and are unfailingly alert. These qualities make the breed an ideal watchdog. As companions, Toy Fox Terriers are the most wonderful little charmers. There's no denying the fact that they are both cute and amusing. It's no wonder that so many people, who've been raised with the breed, feel their family just isn't complete without a Toy Fox Terrier.

Most Toy Fox Terriers are purchased as companions. It's amazing how quickly they become full-fledged members of the family. They adore living in the midst of all the day-to-day goings on and they want to be a part of it all. TFTs become very attached to their families and often demand to be included in all activities. So closely do they identify with the family, that sometimes one wonders if a TFT even realizes that he's a dog! It is the breeds' quick intelligence that wins the Toy Fox Terrier so many admirers. Nowhere is this more apparent than with the house dog. Since he bonds so intimately with the

TFTs are ideal companions. "PR" Meadowood's Jillian and "PR" Casas Adobe's Amber keep Judy Guilot, of Tucson, Arizona, company. (David Ring photo)

14

family, your Toy Fox Terrier will learn to "read" you. Experts tell us that dogs respond more to tone of voice than to words. However, you'll quickly learn that your TFT has learned to recognize certain words and clearly understands their meaning. Say "walk" and you'll find your dog waiting for you at the door. Most Toy Fox Terriers enjoy riding in the car. The minute he hears the word, he'll probably jump up excitedly, eager to go along. Some owners have tried spelling out the letters "c-a-r," in an attempt to fool their dogs. The Toy Fox Terrier, however, quickly figures out this ruse.

Like all toy dogs, the Toy Fox Terrier readily adapts to the ways of your family. If your household tends to be noisy and excitable, your dog is apt to be noisy, too. In a relaxed and quiet household, chances are the dog will respond in a similar fashion. One must realize, however, that with his terrier background, the Toy Fox Terrier is an animated, energetic dog. Those looking for a very quiet, mellow dog would be happier with a less dynamic breed.

Be forewarned, your Toy Fox Terrier will think he should share everything in your life. Typically, he'll prefer to sleep on your bed. If you have a midnight snack, your TFT will think he's entitled, too. You'll discover that he has abundant intelligence and is eager to please. At the same time, however, you'll learn that he has a mind of his own. He will probably challenge you to see just what he can get away with. You'll have to discipline him. Even so, you may wonder, after a time, if you own your Toy Fox Terrier or if it's the other way around!

Very often, Toy Fox Terriers become one-person or one-family dogs. Some individuals seem to have the same degree of love and devotion for the entire family. However, it's not unusual for a TFT to single out one family member as his own special person. Indeed, most Toy Fox Terriers become intensely loyal. For this reason, your dog may not respond eagerly to strangers. While some dogs will greet visitors enthusiastically, others don't care about anyone but their owners. Many TFTs simply won't lavish affection on a person they don't know. You should train your dog to accept visitors admitted to your home. After all, you do want him to act properly. However, it may be best for the visitor to wait for the dog to make the approach, rather than forcing the contact. Many Toy Fox Terriers like to stand back and size up people before coming to them. As long as the visitors act properly themselves, all will go well. However, let them do something that the dog considers improper, and your TFT is likely to raise a ruckus.

As we've said, your Toy Fox Terrier will consider himself a member of the family. He'll consider it his duty, therefore, to protect you from all intruders. With the TFT's keen sense of hearing and his abundant courage, he makes an ideal watchdog. Indeed, he's a four-legged burglar alarm. He'll spring to attention and run to the door the minute he hears a car in the driveway or someone approaching the door. For his size, the TFT has a big bark and he won't stop as long as something is amiss. Many burglars find it far more desirable to rob a house without such a vigilant and noisy alarm.

TFTs love to be close to their owners, as demonstrated by "PR" Cornwell's Heather and owner, Chet Cornwell, of Aripeka, Florida.

The Toy Fox Terrier may be a toy dog, but you'll never convince him of that! No sissy is he. There's not one fearful bone in that little body. Because of this, TFT owners have to exercise a degree of caution with their dogs. The Toy Fox, as we have seen, will jealously guard his home and his owners. He won't hesitate to confront larger dogs aggressively. One TFT is Alaska even chased bears away from his yard. Therefore, when you take your dog for a walk, particularly if he might encounter other dogs, it's best to have him on leash. This small measure of protection, might well save his life.

This is the Toy Fox Terrier, then. A gay, amusing charmer who is uncommonly devoted to his owner, be it one person or an entire family. He is bold and self-confident. A Toy Fox Terrier is also proud. With his flashy colors and sleek good looks, he struts around like he's ready to take on the world. He is also an energetic, lively, sparkling toy dog who greets each day with enthusiasm and a zest for living. His cocky, daring manner and deep loyalty is what makes people so fond of the breed. He's an animated bundle of love, with the spirit of a tiger, on four little legs.

3

The Official U.K.C. Standard

The Official U.K.C. Standard for the Toy Fox Terrier was last revised on January 1, 1982. We thank the United Kennel Club for allowing us to present it here. The numbers, in parentheses, which follow each section of the standard, refer to the diagram that appears at the end of this chapter.

HEAD
Muzzle: Medium long, about same length as skull and somewhat pointed with medium stop. *Faults:* Too narrow. Too much stop. (1)

Nose: Coal black. *Faults:* Brown or pink spotted. (2)

Eyes: Round, dark, prominent, and soft in expression. *Faults:* Too large and bulgy. (3)

Preferred Bite: Teeth should be as nearly as possible together; the points of the upper incisor teeth on the outside of or just overlapping the lower teeth. *Faults:* Overshot—upper teeth overlapping lower teeth by too much. Undershot—lower teeth overlapping upper teeth.

Stop: Medium. (4)

Skull: Slightly rounded. *Faults:* Apple head. (5)

Ears: Pointed V-shaped ears, not too far apart. Placed well up on sides of head. Carried erect. *Faults:* Rounded. Too wide apart. Lop ears. (6)

BODY
Length of body from withers to croup (rump) to equal height from feet to withers. Tapered from rib to flank. Good tuck up. *Faults:* Body too long. Barrelled body.

Neck: Moderately long and slightly arched. (7)

Shoulders: Sloping and well arched. (8)

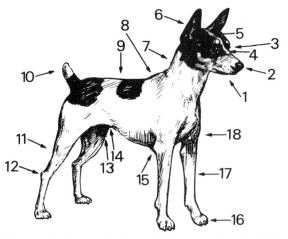

1. Muzzle • 2. Nose • 3. Eyes • 4. Stop • 5. Skull • 6. Ears
• 7. Neck • 8. Shoulders • 9. Back • 10. Tail • 11. Back
Legs • 12. Hock • 13. Stifles • 14. Tuck Up • 15. Elbows
• 16. Feet • 17. Front Legs • 18. Chest

Back: Straight and strong. *Faults:* Sway back. Rounded rump. (9)

Tail: Carried erect, gaily, set high and docked with about a full three-fifths being taken off. *Faults:* No tail. Tail too long. (10)

Back Legs: Strong in thigh, and straight in hock. Stifles turn neither in nor out. *Faults:* Cow hocked. (11)

Hock: Straight. (12)

Stifles: Straight, and turned neither in nor out. (13)

Tuck Up: Moderate.

Elbows: Close to body. Perpendicular with body. *Faults:* Turned in or out. (15)

Feet: Compact and oval rather than round. (16)

Front Legs: Straight and feet pointing forward. *Faults:* Bowed legs. Feet turned out or in. (17)

Chest: Deep chest, fairly well ribbed. *Faults:* Too narrow. Too broad. (18)

Coat: A distinguishing feature of this breed. Short, satiny, and fully textured. Slightly longer at the ruff.

COLOR
Preferred Color: White and black with tan trim, white predominating.

Head: Predominantly black.

Ears: Black on back with very narrow black rim on inner edge.

Trim: Tan on cheeks and/or chops and eye dots.

Face: Without or with a white blaze. A blaze may extend onto either or both sides of lower muzzle. White frost or tiny white spots on lower muzzle are acceptable.

Body: Predominantly white, without or with black spots. White preferably free of speckling (ticks), but permissible to some degree provided white predominates and general good looks are maintained. Tan shading or very small tan spots undesirable, but not faulted.

Acceptable Colors: White and tan or white and black. Color distributed on head and body as for preferred color. White and tan: trim, lighter or darker shade of tan.

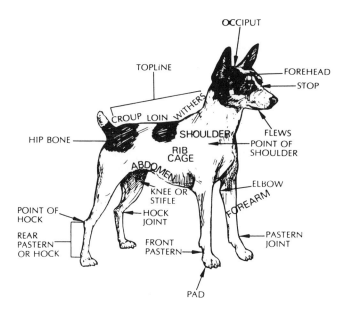

Faults: Any solid color, maltese or chocolate markings. A wide blaze that extends up to the eyes. Black or tan coloring, other than speckling (ticking), on the legs below the knee joint of the front or the hock joint of the hind.

WEIGHT: Not under 3 1/2 lbs., nor over 7 lbs. when fully matured. *Faults:* Overweight. Underweight. Malnourished to make weight limit.

MOVEMENT: Should be smooth and flowing with the legs moving straight, parallel and in the line at a walk or slow trot with the back straight and the tail up. Movement is used to evaluate gait and to evaluate the parts of the body involved in gait.

CHARACTERISTICS OF THIS BREED: Active and lively, yet hardy dogs. Graceful and with much endurance.

DISQUALIFICATIONS: Cryptorchid—no testicle showing at any age group. Monorchid—one testicle showing (not a disqualification until after 6 months of age).

SCALE OF POINTS

Head... 20
Neck... 5
Shoulders.. 10
Chest & Ribs...10
Back & Loins..10
Hindquarters... 10
Elbows.. 5
Legs & Feet... 10
Coat & Color... 10
Stern... 5
Make Up, Coordination and Movement...................... 5

TOTAL POINTS...................................... 100

4

Understanding the Standard

"The Toy Fox Terrier breed has come a long way...We now have many dogs of good type that are excellent specimens of the breed in every respect. Our shows have been a great means of educating breeders and owners as to type, conformation and color and markings..." Dr. E. G. Fuhrman wrote in 1959. He would doubtless be very pleased with the dogs seen in today's show rings. Through the years, there has been a consistent rise in breed quality. Today's dedicated TFT breeders, through careful planning, have sought to move the breed toward the elusive goal of perfection, as expressed in the standard. As always, much work remains to be done. It is hoped that all breeders will strive to better understand the TFT standard.

The standard can be a confusing and mystifying document for the novice. In truth, the standard is simply a word picture that lists the Toy Fox Terrier's essential characteristics. It delineates those qualities that differentiate the TFT from every other breed and it also provides a guideline for the evaluation of individual dogs. The standard assumes that the reader has a basic knowledge of dogs and their structure. It frequently uses terms that are unknown to the novice. The drawings accompanying the Toy Fox Terrier standard will help the novice to understand these terms.

Standards, by their very nature, are brief. While they may be very explicit on some points, such as color and markings, they can't possibly include all the fine nuances that are difficult to express in words. The standard is also flexible. Certainly the breeder or judge cannot ignore the essentials detailed in the standard. There is, however, room for personal interpretation. This is beneficial and important. Dogs are living, breathing animals and each one is an individual. If the Toy Fox Terrier standard minutely detailed every aspect of the breed's appearance, all TFT's would be required to look absolutely alike. Breeders would be expected to produce cookie cutter dogs that looked as though they'd rolled off an assembly line. While, in reality, this would be impossible to achieve, it would also stifle creativity and undermine that search for perfection. Breeders would be intent on producing dogs with the fewest faults, rather than the greatest number of virtues. Novices often learn to "fault judge" first. They quickly learn to detect the presence of mismarks or cowhocks. It takes a more experienced eye to spot the dog with outstanding virtues who, in the end, may make the more worthy contribution to the breed. Therefore, the standard allows breeders to express their own interpretations, as long as they vigilantly comply with the basic requirements.

It is essential for every breeder of Toy Fox Terriers to have an intimate understanding of the standard, which serves as the guideline for the breed. It's not enough to simply read the standard or even to memorize it. Instead, you must understand why it is important for the TFT to have those qualities. The successful breeder is one who reads the standard with an analytical eye, trying to decipher not only its words, but its intent. Novices should study the standard and then view as many TFTs as possible. Don't be afraid to speak to experienced breeders and judges. Once they realize that you have a sincere desire to learn about the breed, they'll be willing to explain their views to you. You'll learn about their personal interpretations and the points that they consider vital in their breeding programs. Their experiences will serve as a guide to obtaining stock and planning your own breeding program.

GENERAL APPEARANCE

A well made Toy Fox Terrier is eye catching. He cannot be faked. There is no profuse coat to conceal his true structure. No trimming or brushing will improve the looks nature gave him. While he's a "toy" and must, therefore, be small, he is also all terrier. He shows the typical, and essential, keen alertness found in all terriers. He's always ready for action, be it a tussle or a romp in the woods. He is full of vim and vigor. Extremely self confident, he gives the impression that he's "full of himself." Self possessed, he radiates energy combined with elegance, and he's absolutely sure that he's equal to any other dog (humans too, perhaps) regardless of size. He acts, looks and moves like an aristocrat. His short, glossy coat and brilliant, rich coloring give him a flashy appearance. His beauty, however, doesn't depend on mere flashiness. All of his body parts combine harmoniously into a smooth whole. The highly held head, the long, finely arched neck, the compact body and the upright tail join to give him a look of poise and balance. Keenly alert, nimbly quick, small, but powerful and built for great endurance, the Toy Fox Terrier wraps it all up in a svelte, elegant package.

Ch. "PR" Currens' Nadine of Parkside, was owned by Doris and the late Howard Currens. Nadine is a lovely example of the breed. Note her balance and typical keen alertness.

THE HEAD

The Toy Fox Terrier's head is the truest indicator of breed type. A typical head is what stamps the dog unmistakably as a TFT. Open a book which features head studies of dogs. As you flip from page to page, you should be able to identify each and every breed by the appearance of the head. Knowing this, the breeders who formulated the standard wisely devoted 20 of the total 100 points to the make-up of the head. They realized that the TFT's alertness, intelligence and character were most clearly seen in the appearance of his head. In past years, head faults in Toy Fox Terriers were common. Dogs with wide-set, rounded ears, bulging eyes, abrupt stops and short noses were common in show rings. With dedication and vigilance, breeders have succeeded in minimizing these faults. While these failings still exist, they are rarely seen on today's winners. While the emphasis on head may seem exaggerated, we must remember that the head is likely to be the first thing seen. The buyer who comes to your house, in search of a pet, will most likely pick a puppy up and look at its' head first. Similarly, as the judge approaches to examine your dog individually in the show ring, the head generally commands his attention first. While it may not seem fair, the dog with a faulty head is likely to be dismissed without a second look. Breeders should beware, however, of becoming obsessed with the head, to the exclusion of the body. A beautiful Toy Fox Terrier head should always be balanced and complemented by a good body. Breeders should concentrate on the "total" dog and not become mere "headhunters."

It is vitally important that the head be in proportion to the rest of the body. A large head, no matter how excellent, will look ridiculous on a small body. Likewise, a tiny head perched on a large body looks ludicrous. The head that would be perfect on a seven pound Toy Fox Terrier, will completely overwhelm a four pound dog. The head must look as though it fits and belongs on the individual dog.

In addition to being in proportion to the body, the head must be proportional itself. The TFT has a very balanced head. The distance from the occiput (the back point of the skull) to the stop (or dividing line between the skull and the muzzle) should equal the distance from the stop to the nose. If these dimensions are unequal, it will mar the head's overall appearance. The best Toy Fox Terrier head will be medium in length and width, with a medium stop.

The Skull

We must, once again, use the words medium or moderate when describing the TFT's skull. A correctly shaped skull is free of exaggeration and should be slightly rounded, rather than flat. The backskull should be moderate in width. A common fault is too broad a backskull, in which the ears are wideset. In addition, the shape of the foreskull, or forehead, has a great influence on TFT

This tiny, 3 pound female has the classic domed, or apple, head. The roundness of her foreskull shows clearly in this photo. Otherwise, her conformation is very nice.

expression. Any tendency toward a bulging or domed foreskull is a very serious fault, indeed. This irregular roundness of the skull is referred to as an "apple head." Apple heads are severely faulted in the show ring, because they destroy true TFT expression. While apple heads may occur in any size TFT, they are more prevalent in very small dogs.

The skull gradually decreases in width to the eyes. The cheeks have a clean-cut leanness. They are relatively flat and muscular, and should not bulge. A Toy Fox Terrier should never look as though he has a chestnut tucked away in his cheeks. Bulging cheek muscles destroy the lean outline of the face. Beneath the eyes there should be moderate fill. The area below the eyes should not drop off drastically.

Ears

"We have better heads on our dogs and there are many more dogs that have natural, erect ears. The ears are very important and they should stand erect. We find that we are gradually getting away from the flop-over of the tip of the ear in the Toy Fox Terrier breed," said Dr. E. G. Fuhrman, in 1959. Indeed, breeders have made strong advances in this area, in recent years. It would be very unusual for a Toy Fox Terrier whose ears were not erect to gain his championship today.

While most TFTs have large ears, it is important that the ears be in proportion to the size of the head. The ears should always be strongly erect. The ear leather (the outer cartilage) should be thin, but with enough strength to keep the ears upright. Thick, heavy ears are more likely to lop over. The ears should always be pointed in a V-shape, rather than rounded. This upright open ear is less prone to infection than a drop ear.

It is difficult to say when a puppy's ears will come up. Generally, the ears on smaller pups come up more quickly than those on larger pups. Stress can also effect ear carriage in young TFT puppies. Ears are likely to go up and down during the teething period. Judges should take this into consideration, when examining puppies. The ears should, however, return to an upright position as the dog matures. Lop or hanging ears are a very serious fault in a mature Toy Fox Terrier. The ears are set rather high on the head. They should, however, not be placed so close together that they touch. The ears must point straight forward so that the entire interior of the ear is visible from the front. The ears should never flair outward or be placed on the side of the head. Ears which are

"PR" Singleton's Thunder Ace, owned by Jeri Singleton, of Annapolis, Maryland has a beautiful head. Note the correct ear set, the beautifully placed eyes and the cleanly chiseled look. (Olan Mills photo)

too widely set greatly detract from the TFTs' alert expression.

Eyes

It is often said that eyes are the mirror of the soul. Indeed, the TFT's eyes do capture much of the breed's character. Those bright, sparkling eyes convey an impression of intelligence and alertness. They are one of the breed's most endearing and charming traits, and at times they seem almost able to talk. When a TFT is excited, his eyes seem full of fire and intensity. When the dog is relaxed, the Toy Fox Terrier has a kind, gentle expression that can melt the hardest heart.

The ideal Toy Fox Terrier eye is round in shape. The round eye does much to soften the TFT's expression. One does occasionally see eyes that are slightly oval in shape, but they must never be small and squinty. The eyes are to be prominent rather than deeply set. However, under no circumstances should the eyes bulge. The bulging eye, which gives a "buggy" appearance, is most likely to be seen in dogs with the undesirable rounded, apple head. This bulging eye is most common today in very small Toy Fox Terriers.

Although it is not mentioned in the standard, the skin fits tightly around the eye. No portion of the third eyelid, or haw, should be visible. When the haw shows, it gives the TFT a "Bloodhound" look that is quite untypical of the breed. The area encircling the eye is dry in appearance and should never have a weepy, tearing look.

The eyes should always be very dark in color. Most breeders prefer an eye as close as possible to black. The iris should fill the eye with no white showing. When white is seen in the corners of the eye, the dog has a look of perpetual surprise that detracts from the keen alertness so desired in TFT expression. A reddish-brown eye color can sometimes be seen in white and tan dogs. However, the darker eye is always preferred. While the standard makes no mention of the eyerims, these should always be black. Flesh colored eyerims, or rims with pink spots, seriously mar the TFT's appearance. Thankfully, this fault is seldom seen.

Stop

The stop is the dividing line between the skull and the muzzle. Generally located just below the eye level, it is the point where the nasal bone and the skull meet. The TFT should have a moderate stop. Too little stop will give a sighthound appearance and may be accompanied by a Roman nose. A far more common fault, particularly in tiny Toy Fox Terriers, is too much stop. This pronounced stop is usually accompanied by an overly short muzzle, and the dog may have the undesirable rounded or apple head as well. Too much stop is a fault to be carefully guarded against, for it destroys true TFT expression.

Muzzle

The TFT's head should gradually taper from the eyes to the nose. The muzzle should be of medium length. While, to some novices, the short muzzle may appear cute, it is entirely wrong for the breed. Often, the short muzzle is accompanied by the round head and pronounced stop. Being a descendant of the Fox Terrier, it is imperative that the shape of the TFT's muzzle suggest strength. The lips should fully cover the teeth, but there should be no excess skin. Hanging, pendant lips, or flews, give the TFT a houndy appearance that is totally incorrect. The lips must always be dry, never drooly.

Nose

The standard calls for a coal black nose. Novices are often astounded when they have their first TFT litter. Newborn pups are born with pink noses, which darken as the pups grow. The noses of some pups seem to turn black overnight, while others become spotted or freckled with black. In most cases, the nose will be fully black by weaning time. No pink spots, however small, are permitted on the nose. Even thought the muzzle surrounding the nose may be white in color, the nose should still be jet black. Light colored noses are seldom a problem in TFTs, but they can occur. In the white and tan TFT, liver colored noses are sometimes seen. No allowance is made for this, however, and any color other than coal black should be faulted in the show ring. The TFT's nostrils should be large and open. Tiny pinched nostrils, which may impair breathing, will hinder endurance and are untypical and incorrect.

The Bite

The "Preferred Bite," as described in the Toy Fox Terrier standard, is commonly known as a "scissors bite." Since the standard does not specifically refer to the scissors bite, by name, there has been some confusion on this portion of the standard. This desired bite, in which the teeth enmesh tightly, is the strongest type of dental alignment. It allows the dog to grasp an object firmly and hold on. When we remember that, early on, Toy Fox Terriers often dispatched rats in rural barns, we'll be able to see the significance of a good, tight scissors bite. Clearly, it takes a good, strong bite to hold a squirming rat.

In addition, the teeth should be strong. The canine teeth, sometimes called the tusks or fangs, should be especially prominent and well-formed. Between them sit the six smaller incisor teeth. Ideally, these should sit in a straight line and not be overly crowded. However, in toy dogs, these teeth can sometimes be slightly out of alignment. While this is not the ideal, it should not be faulted if the bite itself is a good scissors fit.

Level bites do occur in Toy Fox Terriers. In a level bite, the front teeth (the incisors) of the upper and lower jaws meet exactly. While a level bite is certainly preferable to an undershot or overshot bite, it is far less efficient than a scissors bite. Since the upper teeth "ride" on the lower teeth, as the dog ages, the teeth will erode and wear down. By the time the dog is several years old, all that will remain are shards of the original teeth. As the canine teeth are still in basic alignment, the dog will have more grasping power than with an undershot or overshot bite. However, because the teeth don't hold up as well, the standard gives preference to the more sound scissors bite. Care should be taken when breeding dogs with level bites. Some breeders have discovered that dogs with level bites are more prone to producing undershot bites in subsequent generations.

In the undershot bite, the teeth of the lower jaw project beyond those of the upper jaw. In an extremely pronounced underbite, the teeth may even be visible when the the mouth is closed. Many years ago, underbites were a frequently found fault in Toy Fox Terriers. I can recall sitting at ringside and seeing noticeable underbites. Undershot jaws give the TFT a "bulldog" type appearance that is totally foreign to the breed. Since undershot bites are inherited, breeders must take special care to eliminate such dogs from their breeding programs. I have always sold puppies with underbites as pets without papers.

The overshot bite is the exact opposite of the undershot. In this case, the upper jaw overlaps and does not touch the front teeth of the lower jaw. While overbites are not common in the Toy Fox Terrier, they can occur and should be guarded against. The overshot bite has little power and grasping ability. A dog with an overshot jaw has an uncharacteristically weak expression. When the dog is viewed in profile, the lower jaw appears to lack substance and finish.

When evaluating the bites on puppies, beware of discarding a pup with a slight overbite. The lower jaw grows out more slowly than the upper jaw and, in most cases, as the puppy matures the bite will develop into a proper scissors bite. A pronounced overbite, however, is not likely to correct. Undershot bites seldom, if ever, correct as the puppy grows.

Gr. Ch. "PR" Scherger's Miss Cindy, owned by Mr. and Mrs. James Scherger, of New Riegal, Ohio, has a good blaze. Note the desirable narrow dark rim on the inside of the ears.

Frequently, toy dogs are slow to lose their baby teeth. Therefore, it's not uncommon to see a young dog with a double row of teeth. Generally, the puppy teeth loosen and fall out before six months of age. However, some teeth stubbornly remain in place. While some veterinarians will remove these extra teeth, others prefer to wait until the dog reaches a year of age. Since it's often necessary to anesthetize the dog to remove the teeth, many vets feel it is risky to perform this operation on a young pup. Some judges find these double teeth objectionable. However, if the bite is in proper scissors alignment, the dog should not be penalized.

Occasionally, a Toy Fox Terrier may have lost a tooth or two. Since the TFT's mouth is so small, special care must be taken in keeping the teeth clean and free of tartar. Without such care, the TFT may well lose some of his teeth. However, teeth can be lost in other ways, too. Some TFTs are accomplished jumpers and climbers. Indeed, some Toy Fox Terriers act as though they are part mountain goat. An accidental spill may cause a TFT to lose a tooth. A fight between two TFTs can also result in the loss of a tooth. Once again, if the jaw is properly aligned, this should not be a cause for faulting an otherwise good dog.

Head Color and Markings

The standard clearly describes the color and markings to be found on the Toy Fox Terrier's head. In the preferred color (white, black and tan), the head should be predominantly black. The black should be clear and rich, without the presence of white or brown hairs. However, white frosting or tiny spots on the lower muzzle are acceptable.

The TFT is permitted to have a white blaze. A blaze is a white stripe running down the face, between the eyes. Some breeders prefer dogs without blazes. Blazes can make a visual difference in the appearance of the head. The all black head gives the muzzle a shorter appearance, while a white blaze causes the muzzle to appear somewhat longer. The blaze should never be so wide that it touches the eyes or ears. Breeders prefer a symmetrical, properly centered blaze. Off-center blazes are acceptable, however, and should not be penalized, as long as they are not wide enough to touch the eyes.

In newborn puppies, the blaze often appears too wide, and may even touch the eyes or ears. As the pup matures, however, the blaze will diminish in width. Generally, by the time the pup is two to four months old, it will have assumed its final appearance. Similarly, a speck of white or a small streak on the forehead may disappear entirely or diminish to a few white hairs as the puppy grows.

There are some common marking faults found in most lines of Toy Fox Terriers. A blaze may be too wide, actually touching the eyes and ears. Sometimes one side of the face or the majority of the head will be completely white. This mismark is a serious fault and is heavily penalized in the show ring.

The white on the back of this puppy's head actually touches the ears. This is considered a mismark.

The TFT has tan trim over the eyes and on the cheeks. The tan over the eyes appears as small dots or seeds of color. These should be distinctly tan, without interspersed black hairs. The amount of tan trim on the cheeks varies from dog to dog. The color of the trim may vary from a faded, light flaxen to a rich, clear tan. Most breeders and judges prefer the brilliant rich tan that makes such a lovely accent. Some breeders describe this rich tan as mahogany in color. In newborns, the tan markings on the head are truly tiny. However, they grow in size as the pup

This puppy's blaze is too wide. Note that it touches the eye.

develops and, by weaning time, you'll clearly see the desired trim. In white and tans, the accent trim will be less apparent. In well marked white and tans, however, you'll be able to detect a trim of either a lighter or darker color on the cheeks. You must look closely at white and tans to see this subtle accent.

The Toy Fox Terrier's ears should be a clear coal black on the back side. An outline or edging of black should rim the inner edge of the front part of the ear. White on the back of the ears, or any white shading is considered a mismark and should be penalized in the show ring. Sometimes you will see tan hairs blended with the black on the backs of the ears. While not as serious as white spotting, this is still a fault as, in time, the ears usually fade to brown. This is a fairly common fault and breeders should try to eliminate it from their breeding programs. Dogs with pronounced tan trim may show some tan hairs at the base of the inside of the ears. This is permissible and, unless excessive, should not be penalized.

BODY

A well-balanced look is essential to a good Toy Fox Terrier. In general shape, the TFT has a square look. The height from the bottom of the feet to the withers (highest point of the shoulders) should appear approximately equal to the length from the dog's shoulder to his rump. Breeders must always strive for moderation and balance. Many years ago, we saw varying body types in the breed. Overly cobby dogs with broad chests, short legs and no tuck up were common. They might be standing next to a dog of the "deer" type, who was overly tall, with spindly bone, a narrow chest, long body and exaggerated tuck up. Thankfully, we rarely see such extremes any more. A beautifully proportioned Toy Fox Terrier, who at the same time embodies strength and elegance, is what we strive for today.

Some variation is still seen in body length. A too short back, although rare, makes the body appear chunky. This is most undesirable, as it gives the dog a sausage-like appearance. More common is the longer body. Dogs with longer bodies often lack width, which destroys the desired strong appearance. Some breeders are apt to allow a little more body length in a bitch, in the belief that it will give her more room to carry puppies. However, if her body length is such that it detracts from the square appearance, she should be faulted.

The Toy Fox Terrier's amount of bone and length of leg should also be proportional and balanced. A short, stocky body carried on long, spindly legs appears ludicrous. Likewise, a long, slender body supported on short, sturdy legs is not pleasing to the eye. The legs must be proportionate, to correctly balance and carry the body. The Toy Fox Terrier should have a moderate amount of bone. Heavily boned dogs do occur, but are not common. You're more likely to see a dog with insufficient, spindly bone. TFT puppies often appear to have somewhat heavier bone when they are young. The bone will consolidate and be proper as the puppy grows. Beware of the puppy who seems to have slight bone when he's young. Almost always, he'll be too finely boned when he matures.

Forequarters

The forequarters, or front assembly, is the most difficult part of the body to understand and explain. The neck, shoulders, ribs, chest and front legs are all interrelated. If one of these individual parts is faulty, it tends to throw the whole front assembly out of kilter. It is for this reason that faults in the forequarters are the most difficult to eradicate from a breeding program. While a poor rear may often be corrected in a single generation, faults of the front assembly often take many breedings to correct. It takes careful study, evaluation and comparison of dogs to understand fully the requirements for a properly proportioned and angulated front assembly. Faults in the forequarters often show up in motion. We'll take each of the parts of the forequarters in order and attempt to explain their relationship to each other.

Neck

The neck is something more than a mere support for the head. The neck should be clean, muscular and rather long. There should be a slight arch. The elegant, strong neck is very important in the TFT. We must remember that, in the past, the Toy Fox Terrier was used for ratting. He had to have ample length of neck to quickly grab the rat, without lowering his body. He also needed sufficient strength to shake his head from side to side, breaking the rat's neck. This takes flexibility and power. While your TFT isn't likely to be employed as a rat catcher today, you will often see him take one of his toys and shake it in a similar manner.

The neck should be clean, without excessive throatiness. There should be no hanging folds of extra skin. Thin, spindly necks lack power and should be faulted. Similarly, short heavy necks, where the head appears to perch on the shoulders, detract from the TFT's appearance and are structurally incorrect. The neck should have a slight arch. Rigidly straight necks, which lack flexibility, should be faulted. Also the

Gr. Ch. "PR" Singleton's Stormy Ace, owned by Jeri Singleton, shows ideal shoulder conformation. Note the lovely flowing lines, as the neck blends into the shoulder blades and cleanly melds into the topline. In addition, this dog's front and rear angulation match perfectly, giving him a well balanced look.

concave, or ewe-neck, is a serious fault and is usually accompanied by a too straight shoulder. With the desired slight arch, the Toy Fox Terrier holds his

31

head high and shows the alert confidence that's so typical of the breed.

The neck should widen gradually to the shoulders. An elegant neck blends smoothly into well laid back shoulders. It should be noted that there are the same number of vertebrae in the neck of a dog that appears short necked as in one with the correct length. The position of the shoulder blades and their degree of angulation contributes visibly to the appearance of neck length. The neck on a dog with steep, upright shoulders begins further up the vertebrae than the dog with properly sloping shoulders. This creates a short-necked look. An elegant neckline, which slopes smoothly into properly placed shoulders, makes for a stylish appearances in the show ring and greatly enhances your TFT's appearance.

Shoulders

The shoulder blades should be long, sloping and well laid back. When you feel the withers (the highest point of the shoulders) you should be able to tell that the shoulder blades are placed close together. Look at the dog in profile. If you see one smooth, continuous line extending from the neck, past the shoulder blades, without a rise or dip, the dog most likely has very good shoulders. There should never be an abrupt break where the neck and the shoulders join. Similarly, a dip in the back, behind the shoulders blades, usually

An extremely poor TFT, with more faults than you can count. Note the very wide facial blaze. The dog lacks overall balance and appears rangy. He does not have sufficient depth or width of chest, and appears to be perched on stilts.

indicates insufficient lay-back. The ideal shoulder layback allows the dog to extend his front legs with maximum reach. When viewed from the side, the legs should swing freely in a straight line from the shoulders (i.e., there should be no break at the elbow or foot). Straight shoulders are seen fairly often in Toy Fox Terriers, and breeders should strive for better, more correct lay-back.

Chest and Ribs

The Toy Fox Terrier has a deep chest and well defined ribs. When viewed from the side, the brisket, or forepart of the chest, should extend to or just above the elbow. A TFT with inadequate depth of brisket appears to be unduly leggy, as though he were perched on stilts. When viewed from the front, the chest should be wide enough to enable the legs to stand parallel to each other.

The well-sprung rib cage is neither too narrow (slab-sided) nor too wide (barrel-shaped). The proper oval-shaped rib cage greatly enhances endurance, a key characteristic of the Toy Fox Terrier. The circumference of the chest will narrow somewhat behind the elbows. This allows the dog clearance in bringing his front legs back. The barrel-chest cannot expand as freely when the dog exerts himself. This fault is often accompanied by an overly wide, Bulldog-like, chest. In motion, the barrel chested dog cannot get his front legs back behind him. Instead, they hit the chest and cause interference. In order to avoid this, the elbows are often forced out. Barrel chested dogs usually have too much width between the tops of the shoulder blades. The slab-sided dog is apt to be short on endurance, too. The lungs, contained in the rib cage, must be able to expand as the dog

Nat. Gr. Ch. "PR" Gorden's Toy Rooster, owned by Doug and Betty Gorden, of Crosby, Texas, shows a correct front assembly. Note the straight front, good width of chest and proper length of neck.

runs. If there's not enough room for this to occur, endurance will be hampered.

Front Legs

The front legs should drop straight from the elbows to the feet. They should be the same distance apart at the elbow as at the feet. For this to happen, the chest must be moderately wide. When the chest is too wide, the legs are usually forced "out at the elbows." This fault gives a very coarse, clumsy, Bulldog-like appearance and is to be heavily penalized. A too narrow chest allows the dog to bring his elbows together under his body. This, too, should be faulted in the show ring. French fronts, Chippendale fronts or east west fronts occur when the legs turn outward below the pasterns. This loose, unsound front is often found and should be faulted. The old style TFT was overly broad and coarse, and frequently was out at the elbows. While breeders have greatly reduced these faults, they can still be found and should be penalized.

The pasterns should appear straight, strong and flexible. They should be nearly perpendicular to the ground. There is actually a very slight slope to the pasterns which helps cushion the feet and absorb shock. There should be a slight "give" or springiness to the pasterns, but they must, under no circumstances, be sloped. This is called "down in the pasterns" and is a serious and ugly fault.

Feet

Often, people make the mistake of overlooking the feet. And yet, poor feet can spoil the TFT's overall appearance. Large, splayed, thin feet will mar the look of the most beautiful dog. Good feet are functional, too. Being a long lived and active breed, it's important that the feet hold up throughout the dog's lifetime.

Toy Fox Terriers have "hare" feet. In this type of foot, the two middle toes are longer than the outside toes. The feet should be compact. Splayed feet, in which the toes spread, are apt to be faulted in the show ring, although not specifically identified as a fault in the standard. Proper care of the nails will help to prevent splaying. When nails become overly long, they cause the toes to spread. The pads should be thick enough to cushion the feet and absorb shock.

The TFT always has dewclaws on the front legs and may have them on the rear legs. Since the standard makes no mention of the dewclaws, breeders are free to exercise their own discretion in leaving or removing them. Some breeders feel that removing the front dewclaws gives the legs a cleaner appearance. Most breeders do remove the rear dewclaws. These rear appendages are likely to be more prominent and therefore are more liable to injury. Since the hind dewclaws are more prominent and may stick out, the TFT may look as though he is moving closer in the rear.

This female has an extremely faulty front. This is a classic example of a dog that is "out at the elbows." In addition, her ears are set too wide and flair out to the side. If you look closely, you'll also see that her tail was docked too long.

Topline

The TFT's topline should be straight and strong. When we look at the whole body, we can see why a strong back and topline is essential. The spinal vertebrae act as a bridge which supports the head and neck, as well as the weight of the ribs and body organs. They connect the forequarters to the hindquarters. Therefore, it is essential that the back is strong and taut. The length of the back is influenced by the proper lay of the shoulders. A dog with steep, upright shoulders, which are carried too far forward, will appear to have a longer back than the dog with correct shoulder angulation.

Most judges seriously fault sway or dippy backed dogs, or those with roached backs. Dogs that are "high in the rear" are also severely faulted. Rightly so, for these faults totally mar the dog's overall appearance. Judges must take care in assessing toplines in the show ring. When the dog is posed, many topline faults can be concealed. By pulling the rear legs back farther than normal, a mildly swayed back can be made to appear level. Also, by stacking the hind legs farther apart than normal, the high in the rear look can be disguised. However, once the dogs move, such subterfuges fail, for the faults can easily be seen.

Underline

The Toy Fox Terrier's belly should be moderately tucked up. This gentle rise contributes much to the appearance of elegance and agility. An extreme tuck up is incorrect, however. Too much tuck up gives a Greyhound appearance. It is generally coupled with an arch or roach of the loin and, often, with a low tail set. This is clearly at odds with the strong, level back called for in the standard.

Ch. "PR" Hopkins' Jeff's Janice, owned by Hopkins Kennel, illustrates the correct, strong topline.

Hindquarters

The Toy Fox Terrier has a strong and muscular rear. For his size, he is quite powerful. The upper thighs are broad and muscular, but not beefy. Excessively muscled thighs appear coarse and bunchy. When viewed from behind, the legs, hocks and feet should be straight. The hocks are low and strong, and must always be perfectly upright. They should point neither in nor out. Cowhocks, in which the hocks turn inward toward each other, is a common fault and should be severely penalized in the show ring.

Some confusion has resulted from the description of "stifles" in the standard. "Stifles: straight, and turned neither in nor out," refers to the stifles as seen from the rear. While no mention is made of rear angulation, most breeders and judges agree that the TFT has a slight to moderate bend of stifle when viewed from the side. Since the rear is the source of the dog's drive and power when moving, moderate angulation allows the dog to step out with a free and easy stride. The overly angulated rear often tends to be weaker and gives the dog a crouched appearance in the rear. Straight stifles are equally faulty for they restrict the dog's movement. The straight stifled dog moves with a stilted, stick-like action. Sometimes it can be difficult for the judge to accurately gauge the bend of stifle in the Toy Fox Terrier. Many an adequately angulated TFT will tense his muscles, when posed in the show ring, giving the appearance of being straight stifled. Dogs that are particularly showy and keyed up, in the ring, often display this tenseness. In such a case, the judge should try to catch the dog in a more relaxed moment and pay close attention when he gaits.

Tail

While the standard faults a dog for having no tail or a tail too long, the most important element, for the breeder, is the placement and carriage of the tail. Next to the head, the tail is the most expressive part of the Toy Fox Terrier.

Gr. Ch. "PR" Byrd's Mi-Treasure, owned by Ronald and Colleen Byrd, of Berger, Missouri, a lovely TFT. Although one of her rear legs is extended farther back than normal, you can still see the appearance of strength.

That little stub of a tail has a language all its own. An upright tail bespeaks a bold, confident and alert nature. A TFT with his tail glued to his bottom looks as though he is cringing, fearful or not feeling well. The Toy Fox Terrier is a cocky little breed and his upright tail demonstrates his innate self-confidence and sense of importance. A TFT who carries his tail low appears shy and fearful.

The tail must be set very high. It should be directly on the level of the back and carried upright. The set-on of the tail is very important. While a TFT's show ring appearance may be marred by an incorrectly docked tail, an improper tail-set may be passed on to the next generation. The tail is an extension of the back's vertebrae. When a TFT has a low-set tail, the back has a squatty, roach-like appearance and may appear longer. In motion, the Toy Fox should carry his tail bolt upright. Sometimes we see dogs whose tails curl over and lay on the back. Some judges penalize this "too" gay tail. However, it is preferable to the undesirable low set tail.

Naturally bobbed tails are found in some lines of Toy Fox Terriers. These shortened tails can present problems for the show breeder. Some "natural bobs," as they are called, are born with no tail at all. Natural bob litters often contain pups with tails of varying lengths. Rarely are natural bobs born with tails of the exactly desirable length. This can make docking difficult for the person dreaming of future champions. Clearly, if the breeder subtracts the full three-fifths called for in the standard, they'll have a tail that is too short for the show ring. In a later chapter, I've included tips for docking natural bob tails to an appropriate length.

Some breeders, particularly those who don't like tail docking, value and include the natural bobs in their breeding programs. Due to the difficulty in assessing correct length, many other breeders prefer to exclude natural bobs from their kennels. In years past, the "NB," or natural bob designation was included after the dog's registered name, and could be clearly seen on pedigrees. Since 1982, however, the NB designation now appears after the dog's color, on the registration papers. Therefore, it does not appear on current pedigrees. This can make tracing the prevalence of natural bobs difficult, although it will still appear beside the names of dogs registered prior to November, 1982.

Coat

The TFT's short, satiny coat is one of the breed's most distinctive features. A Toy Fox Terrier's physical condition is generally reflected by the condition of his coat. Parasites, both internal and external, can cause the coat to become rough, dry and dull. The coat of a TFT, in good condition, appears shiny and is soft to the touch. The skin should be firm, but pliable. The hair is short and rather fine in texture. It should never be coarse, long or wiry. The hair should be thick enough to cover the body well. The coat, however, is finer and sparser on the insides of the legs and on the belly. The coat can be slightly longer on the back of the neck and shoulders. One of the pleasures of the TFT coat is its' ease of maintenance. With an occasional bath and a light brushing, your TFT will always look his best.

Body Color and Markings

Many people are struck by the flashy coloring of the Toy Fox Terrier. Proper color and markings are easily seen at a glance, in the show ring. Indeed, novices often place undue emphasis on the portion of the standard relating to color and markings. While proper color and markings are undeniably important, breeders must beware of placing so much emphasis on markings that they forget about the "total" dog. It is certainly true, however, that correct markings can do much to add to the beauty of a good TFT.

The TFT standard allows for three acceptable color combinations. The preferred color, and the one most often seen in the show ring, is composed of white and black with tan trim. (To most accurately describe color, TFT breeders should always place the predominate color first when

A dog with a very poor topline. Note the roached back and excessive tuck-up. In addition, this natural bob dog has no tail.

describing their dogs.) The white, black and tan is the most striking and flashiest looking of the TFT's color combinations and, therefore, the one vastly preferred by most breeders. Also acceptable are white and tan or white and black TFTs. Any solid color or any other colored markings are considered serious faults. While solid colors and dogs with maltese, or blue coloration are rightly listed as faults in the standard, such coloration is rarely seen in today's TFT.

As we have seen, primarily white body color has been a hallmark of the Fox Terrier since the late 1700's. For this reason, primarily white color became an early requirement in the TFT standard. The white on the Toy Fox Terrier should be a pure, clean white, much like the color of freshly

Ch. "PR" Kadelon's Carmelle, owned by Bernice McDermitt, of Wapakoneta, Ohio, is an excellent white and tan TFT.

fallen snow. The white must not have a cream, biscuit or ivory tinge. The dog's body and leg area must be at least one-half white. Any deviation from this is seriously penalized in the show ring.

Solid black or solid tan markings which run down the legs to the feet are considered mismarks and are heavily faulted in the ring. Any distinct spot of black or tan, located below the elbows on the front legs or below the hock joints on the rear legs, should be severely faulted. In a TFT with a black spot on the hip or the rump, in which the color extends under the tail, a tiny spot of tan is sometimes noted on the rectum. This should not be penalized, unless there is an excessive amount of tan color. Likewise, shoulder spots sometimes extend down the upper portion of the leg above the elbow. Very often there will appear a coin-sized spot of tan on the upper leg. Such a tiny spot may also appear when a black marking overlaps the bottom of the rib cage. With regard to these spots, the standard says, " Tan shading or very small tan spots undesirable, but not faulted." It can be clearly seen from this statement that these markings, if not excessive, should not be faulted in the show ring. Generally, these are only occasional occurrences. Such markings, although not to be penalized, are undesirable and breeders should seek to eliminate them from their breeding programs.

The standard also permits some ticking. Ticking, or speckling, is a small area of colored hair found on the white background. Through selective breeding, ticking has been minimized, but you can still find TFTs with some speckling. While ticking is not desirable, dogs with otherwise good markings should not be heavily penalized for its presence. Under faults, the standard states: "Black or tan coloring, other than speckling (ticking), on the legs below

38

the knee joint of the front or the hock joint of the hind." While this should be clearly explanatory, it has been noted that some judges have penalized dogs with ticking below the knee or hock joints. This portion of the standard was specifically intended to penalize dogs with solid color marks running down the legs, below these joints, *not* dogs with ticking.

While markings on the head may be difficult to assess for the breeder whelping his first Toy Fox Terrier litter, body markings are easier to determine. The spots of color on the body will grow and expand as the pup develops. The tan, which may line a black spot or markings running down the leg, may be barely visible or appear minimal in the newborn. However, by the time the pup is two to three months old, they will become evident.

White and tan dogs, and white and black dogs are acceptable in the TFT. A good white and tan dog is very attractive, but not as flashy looking as the white, black and tan Toy Fox Terrier. In truth, properly marked white and tan TFTs are more difficult to breed than the preferred color. White and tan dogs, just like their preferred color counterparts, should have at least half the background body color in white. Over half of the head must be tan. In white and tan TFTs, breeders must beware of using dogs which are white and liver or white and chocolate brown. These are not true white and tans and often have pink or liver colored noses. This, of course, is a fault in any color of TFT, for the nose should be totally black. A few breeders have succeeded in gaining championships on white and tan dogs. We hope that they will continue in their efforts to breed well-marked white and tans, with good conformation

MOVEMENT

Some owners are apt to place little importance on the movement of the Toy Fox Terrier. After all, this is a toy breed, they say, not a hunting dog that spends all day in the field. Anyone who's lived with a TFT, however, can attest to the fact that he is a vital, active dog. Indeed, as he runs around the house, jumping from chair to chair and from lap to lap, he may receive more exercise than many larger breeds. The TFT is a long lived breed. With proper conformation and movement, he will remain hardy and vigorous throughout his life.

This puppy has several color faults. His body coloring is predominantly black, not white. Note that the color extends below his hock. In addition, this heavily boned pup is overly large for his age.

It is often said that movement is the truest indicator of good conformation. There is something to be said for this, as gaiting is a good measure of overall soundness. Proper gait just isn't possible without proper conformation and structure. Many faults that may not be apparent when the dog is posed, come quickly to light when the dog is moved. If you went to purchase a used car, you would not be content to merely look at it, no matter how close your examination. You'd insist on taking the car for a test drive, because you'd be more likely to feel or hear some defect. Likewise, when the dog moves, you may well see some fault that had previously escaped your notice.

In the show ring, the gait is examined from three angles. The judge will look at the dog from the side, in profile, as he gaits around the ring. He will also look at the dog from the rear, as he moves away from him, and from the front, while the dog approaches. This gives the judge a balanced view of the dog from every angle and allows him to best assess the TFT's movement. The dog will be expected to "trot," which is the canine's most efficient and natural gait. When a dog walks, three feet are always in contact with the ground. When the dog trots, only two feet touch the ground. The trot is called a two-beat lateral gait, in which opposing diagonals move together. In other words, the right front foot moves at the same time as the left rear foot, and the left front and right rear foot move together. Good physical structure is very important when a dog trots, for in this mode he must rely on speed and balance.

Profile Movement

The gait, as seen in profile, is the most difficult for the novice to properly assess. That's because so many interrelated parts of the body can be seen at the same time. The judge will be looking for a free and easy gait. He'll check the topline to make sure that it stays level when the dog moves. A dog whose back bobs up and down is not an efficient mover. He's wasting his effort with up and down, rather than forward motion.

Balanced angulation is essential to good movement, when viewed in profile. A Toy Fox Terrier whose front and rear angulation are equal will have the proper rhythmic gait. Though a TFT may have poor angulation (too straight in the shoulders and stifles) his gait will still appear more balanced than the dog with mismatched angulation. His gait, however, will not be as efficient and free as the properly angulated dog. The length of his stride will be correspondingly shorter and he'll have to take more steps to cover the same distance. He will lack that beautiful, smooth stride, with good reach and drive, that's so desirable.

Let's think for a moment about the way an automobile operates. Generally, the rear wheels of your car provide the propulsive power that drives the car forward. The front wheels set the course of direction. If your front wheel should sink into a mud hole, the propulsive power from the rear will probably be sufficient to dislodge the vehicle. If the rear wheels should bog down, however, it'll be much more difficult to free the car. If you should suffer a sudden blowout when you're on the highway, you'll have an easier time controlling the car if one of the rear tires goes flat than if a front tire is affected. Since the front wheels are instrumental in controlling direction (steering), a blowout of a front tire, particularly at high speed, creates a dangerous situation. A blowout on the rear may temporarily affect control, but you will likely be able

40

to safely maneuver your car to the side of the road.

Now, let's consider the dog's body as an efficient, car-like machine. His little legs act much like the wheels of our car. The dog generates his power from the rear. Without strong muscular thighs and sufficient angulation, he won't be able to develop the power necessary to effortlessly propel him forward. His front legs, just like the car's front wheels, are responsible for changes in direction. They must have the angulation to enable the dog to make rapid turns and changes of direction. When the dog is ready to stop, the front legs and shoulders must be powerful enough to absorb the initial impact. With proper flexibility and balance, the dog can pull up suddenly, abruptly and appear to "stop on a dime."

This young TFT is primarily white, but her black coloration extends down her front leg. Such markings are faulted in the show ring.

The judge hopes to see free and effortless movement. He'll be paying attention to the dog's length of stride. He wants to see the rear legs reach well under the dog, then straighten out, driving the dog forward, and follow through vigorously. This long stride will provide the maximum in power. He'll want to see the front legs reach smoothly forward from the shoulder, without breaking the straight line from shoulder to foot. The foot must then hit the ground smoothly, drive backward and follow through, although the front follow through should not extend as far as the rear. It's important that the front legs be able to keep up with those driving rear legs. If the front stride does not match that of the rear, it causes interference. This, of course, makes for an inefficient gait and impedes forward movement.

The feet must clear the ground cleanly. The dog should never appear to be tripping over his feet. However, they should *just* clear the ground. Neither the front nor rear feet should be raised abruptly upward. A dog who raises his feet is wasting energy, which should always be directed forward, rather than upward. A dog who flings or kicks his feet upward while gaiting, breaks the clean forward motion we want to see. This inefficient motion tires the dog unnecessarily.

Rear Movement

The judge will want to examine your dog's movement from the rear, to ascertain if his hindquarters move properly. As the dog begins to move, he'll be in a slow trot. At this slower speed, his rear feet should move straight forward. In a dog with a good rear, the hocks will be exactly vertical and moderately apart. If the dog moves with his hocks too wide, he'll have a waddling, duck-like action. If the hocks are too close, particularly if they brush together, they will interfere with the necessary free and easy movement. Either fault robs the dog of power. The hocks should not turn inward, which indicates cowhocks. Sometimes a dog who is minimally cowhocked will have escaped the judge's attention on individual examination. However, as the dog moves, the judge will be able to see that telltale convergence of the hocks. Similarly, the hocks should not turn outward. While this type of action is rarely seen, it should nonetheless be penalized.

As the dog picks up speed and moves into a fast trot, the placement of the feet will change somewhat. As speed increases, the dog has to adjust his foot fall to maintain balance. Therefore, he inclines his feet inward so that they converge on a center line under his body. This convergence is dubbed "single tracking" because the dog's front and rear feet will hit a single centered line. This phenomenon can best be seen on a sandy, damp beach where the dog's pads will leave an imprint. It's also possible to observe this on snow of the proper texture. The next time the opportunity presents itself, try trotting your dog on one of these surfaces. You'll be able to clearly see this center line, single tracking movement as the dog trots.

As we've said, in the fast trot the legs will incline inward. There should be no deviation, however, in that straight unbroken line from the hips to the feet. The feet should still reach straight forward, hocks straight, with no side to side motion. In the good moving dog, with proper angulation, the judge will be able to see the pads of the rear feet on the follow through. This shows the judge that the dog moves powerfully, gets his feet well under him and follows through fully. It's a visible testament to the dog's rear drive.

Front Movement

The judge will also want to see the dog's movement from the front. As we said, when we discussed forequarters, this is the most complicated and interrelated part of the dog's structure. Therefore, the list of front movement faults are extensive and too lengthy to include here. In the very slow trot, the dog's legs should drop straight from the elbows to the feet and be parallel to each other. Just as in rear action, as the dog's speed increases, his front legs will converge on that imaginary center line.

Front movement is dependent on numerous factors in addition to correct shoulder layback. The construction of the rib cage is vitally important. The judge will look for interference in the elbow action. If the dog has a barrel chest, he'll have to swing his elbows wide to avoid the chest. This horrid fault will be immediately apparent. The judge will also be looking for any unusual looseness in the front movement. He'll quickly detect any crossing over or weaving of the front legs, which would point to a loosely constructed shoulder. The judge will be looking at the feet and pasterns, to be sure they reach straight forward. The front feet should neither turn inward nor outward.

A properly moving Toy Fox Terrier is truly beautiful. With his head and tail held high, he steps out cleanly and crisply in a straightforward, efficient manner. All of his body parts join to give him a harmonious, synchronized action. Once we understand the complexities of movement, it is truly amazing to see everything come together to produce that wonderful effortless gait. Good movement in a Toy Fox Terrier should be treasured and cherished, for its a sure indication of a balanced, well made dog.

5

TFT Size

Size has always been a hotly debated topic in TFT circles. As we've discussed in the history chapter, the pioneers in our breed were constantly confronted with disagreements as to proper TFT size. It was only through their never ending vigilance that the Toy Fox Terrier remained a true toy dog. As Dr. Fuhrman reminded breeders, it takes only a short time to increase size. To keep the TFT a toy breed, however, requires continued work on the part of breeders.

The policies of the United Kennel Club have done much to firmly establish the proper size for the Toy Fox Terrier. Before entering any U.K.C. licensed show, each Toy Fox Terrier is weighed. The standard states that the Toy Fox Terrier cannot weigh under 3 1/2 pounds, nor over 7 pounds, when fully mature. The dog must comply with this requirement to be eligible to compete. Allowance is made, of course, for dogs entered in the Puppy and Junior classes. Since they may not have reached full maturity, they are permitted to enter shows, even though they have not yet reached 3 1/2 pounds. In all other classes, the Toy Fox Terrier must fit within the prescribed weight range. Therefore, our dogs' size must remain a major concern for every dedicated TFT breeder.

CONTROLLING SIZE THROUGH DIET

It should go without saying that no breeder should ever try to produce small dogs by limiting the quantity and quality of their feed. In the past, old wives tales held that size could be controlled by underfeeding puppies. We now know that size is determined by genetics. Any attempt to purposely underfeed, starve or malnourish a puppy, to retard growth, is abusive and the practice is never condoned by reputable breeders. Furthermore, the end result is usually a dog which is unsound and weak. We must remember that one of the Toy Fox Terriers' most pleasing qualities is the breed's overall hardiness. A diet which lacks sufficient amounts of vitamins and minerals may lead to conditions such as rickets. This will mar the dog's appearance and affect his health throughout his shortened life. He'll lack the robust vigor that we expect in this breed. Correct size must be maintained through consistent breeding practices, not ruses. Our objective is to produce bright, bouncy, healthy, longlived Toy Fox Terriers. Small size should never be achieved at the expense of type and soundness.

The TFT is a toy dog, as little "PR" Rinebold's Penny shows.

VARIATIONS IN TFT SIZE

Our standard allows for considerable variation in the size of the Toy Fox Terrier. We must consider that the largest dog eligible to compete (7 pounds) is twice the weight of the smallest (3 1/2 pounds). This allows for flexibility in the breed, which can be most beneficial. A more limited weight range would eliminate dogs which excelled in valuable breed characteristics. This wide variation in size, however, can make it difficult for the breeder to predict the size of dogs he can expect in any given litter. Breeding for consistent size is one of the most challenging aspects facing the Toy Fox Terrier breeder.

There can be great variation in the size of TFTs from one bloodline to another. Further, there can be tremendous differences in the size of TFTs in any given bloodline. Greatly varying size may, in fact, be found in a single litter. Let's take a hypothetical litter of three pups. It is quite possible that one will mature very small (under 4 1/2 pounds). Another may, upon maturity, achieve a moderate size of 5-5 1/2 pounds. The third puppy may well mature at 6-7 pounds. All of these dogs have matured within the standard for the breed. At the same time, this is quite a variation within a single litter. When the 5-5 1/2 pound dog is bred, what will he produce? Will he produce his own medium size or that of his smaller or larger siblings? Of course, you'd have to take into account the size of the mate. If, however, the dog that you breed to has an equally diverse mixture of sizes in his genetic background, the result could be anyone's guess. Is it any wonder that breeders can go a little crazy in trying to carefully consider size in their breeding programs?

Adding to the difficulty has been the demand for a variety of sizes by the buying public. You will find that some buyers want the small Toy Fox Terrier that matures at 5 pounds or less. Most buyers, particularly those intent on showing and breeding, seek the TFT that will mature at 5-7 pounds in weight. Indeed, it is unusual to see a TFT weighing less than 4 1/2 pounds who can compete in our larger, highly competitive shows. Some pet buyers, however, honestly prefer the larger TFT, who will ultimately tip the scales at 7-10 pounds. Since Toy Fox Terrier breeders must sell most of their puppies, the public demand for different sizes fosters this variation.

CONTROLLING SIZE IN YOUR BREEDING PROGRAM

How simple it would be if we could breed a 7 pound female to a 5 pound male and be assured of getting a whole litter of 6 pound TFTs. Unfortunately, it just doesn't work that way. Size is controlled by genetics, and that 5 pound TFT is just as likely to produce the size of one of his ancestors as he is his own moderate size. Consistency of size, from generation to generation and from litter to litter, is extremely difficult to produce. If one of the goals of our breeding programs is to produce a majority of dogs that mature within the standard, then it is necessary to try.

What's the best way to achieve consistent size in your breeding program? Unfortunately, there's no easy answer. It will take study, vigilance and, perhaps, a little luck. First, you must learn as much as you possibly can about the dogs listed in your TFT's pedigree. Don't hesitate to ask his breeder what the weights of the parents were. If he can provide you with the weights of the grandparents and great grandparents, so much the better. You might also want to inquire about the weights of the siblings of the dogs listed in your TFT's pedigree. The more information you are armed with, the better chance you will have of estimating the size puppies your dog will produce. If the majority of ancestors in your TFT's background are dogs which fall in the 5-6 pound range, you'll have a better chance of the dog consistently producing this size.

Occasionally one finds a dog who can control size. This type of dog can be invaluable in a breeding program. If you are fortunate enough to find yourself the owner of such a dog, be thankful. It will take some experimentation to determine if you have a dog who is prepotent for producing one size. Remember, Toy Fox Terriers have small litters and it will take several breedings before you will be able to see a definite pattern. The size of the individual dog does not necessarily bear on the ability to control size. It is possible to have a large female who consistently produces small puppies. She is producing the size she's inherited from her ancestors, rather than the size you see. The reverse can also be true. Just because a dog is small, this does not guarantee that he'll produce small puppies.

Nat. Gr. Ch. Parks Toys John Boy, owned by Ruby Klaes, of Galveston, Texas. This 6 pound dog is an ideal size for the TFT.

Should you breed an oversize Toy Fox Terrier? Many breeders do, particularly with females. Often larger TFTs conform beautifully to the standard in all respects but size. Some breeders are firmly convinced that larger bitches will produce larger litters, whelp more easily and nurture stronger puppies. If we are ever to succeed in consistently controlling size within our breeding programs, however, a more logical approach is necessary. Most of us know that breeding very small TFT bitches can be hazardous to the bitch's health. However, normal size TFT bitches are certainly capable of producing strong, healthy litters.

Let's look at the question of size, in light of the standard. While the Toy Fox Terrier standard lists only one official disqualification (monorchid or cryptorchid dogs), there are actually two disqualifiers. Since oversized or undersized dogs are not permitted to be shown, size is, in effect, a disqualification. The standard does, of course, list a number of faults. Some breeders would never dream of breeding a TFT that was not primarily white in color. They might even shy away from breeding a dog with a serious mismark. And yet, that same breeder will often breed an oversized bitch. This isn't logical, but it happens regularly. There are some times when breeding an oversize TFT is necessary, of course. If the dog is the last of a particular bloodline that you're working with, and he happens to be oversize, then it may well be worth breeding him despite his size.

I don't wish to get on a soapbox on the issue of size. Each TFT breeder will have to use his discretion and make up his own mind about whether to breed oversize dogs. Rather, I would like to share with you my personal experiences. In all honesty, many years ago, when my husband, Phil, and I first began breeding Toy Fox Terriers, we occasionally bred some oversized dogs. We quickly discovered, however, that once size was introduced into a kennel, it became extremely difficult to eradicate. It was very frustrating to produce a litter of puppies, choose a promising one to retain for show and breeding, only to have it mature over the standard. For the last 15-20 years, I've made a conscientious effort to control size within my kennel. Personally, I prefer all my Toy Fox Terriers to weigh in at 5 1/2 to 6 1/2 pounds. I know that some breeders prefer slightly smaller or larger dogs. I began restricting my breedings to dogs that fell within my preferred weight range. I am the first to admit that achieving consistency has not been easy. However, I do feel that I have made progress toward reaching my goal. I do still have dogs which mature out of my preferred weight. I also have an occasional dog that's over or undersized. However, the incidence of these cases has lessened and most of my dogs now fall within my preferred weight range. I admit that the battle is not yet won. It will take continued work to achieve the consistency I desire. I do feel, however, that I have made great strides in establishing this quality in my kennel.

I do have one problem, now that I have monitored dogs so rigorously for size. On occasion, it is necessary for me to purchase a stud, from outcross lines, to supplement my breeding program. Since most breeders don't select as stringently for size as I do, difficulties may arise. I may, inadvertently, be introducing greater size into my kennel through the purchase. The only thing to do is try to obtain as much information as possible about the stud being purchased. Then, I cross my fingers and hope that, when bred to my bitches, he produces the size puppies I want.

I do wish that more breeders would pay strict attention to size in the Toy Fox Terrier. However, I make no judgments against those who don't share my view. I hope only that those who might be interested in trying to control size, within their breeding programs, may benefit from my experiences in the same endeavor.

ESTIMATING ADULT SIZE

Novices often ask how they can determine the size their puppies will reach at maturity. There are no pat answers. Different bloodlines mature at different rates. Dogs from some bloodlines take longer to mature than those from others. There may even be occasional variations within one bloodline. In general, my pups usually stop growing by the time they're around nine months of age. Even my 3-5 year old dogs seldom weigh over 1/2 pound more than their nine month weight.

This is the formula I use to estimate the weight the puppy will ultimately reach. I figure an average weight gain of one pound per month until six months of age. After this point, weight gain slows considerably. In my bloodline, I've found that a puppy who weighs 5 1/2 or 6 pounds at six months of age will rarely weigh over 7 pounds when fully mature.

The puppies that will eventually fall within my preferred weight range,

A TFT that just kept growing. This dog matured at 21 pounds! This may be a "throwback" to the TFT's Fox Terrier ancestry.

usually weigh about 1 1/2 pounds at six weeks of age. This may vary by 1/4 pound either way. When these preferred weight puppies reach six months of age, they generally average 5 1/2 to 6 pounds. This is just the size I want. Naturally, if they weigh less than this amount, they will reach a smaller size at maturity and if larger, they'll mature into bigger TFTs. Like all breeders, I have had a few exceptions. Once in a while, I'll have a puppy which matures very quickly or one that grows at a slower rate. Still, puppies which followed this general guideline have rarely exceeded the standard.

There are a few other indicators of ultimate size at maturity. I will pass along these tips, which I use, although they might not provide much insight to the novice with his first litter. Much will depend on how many litters of TFT puppies you've seen. It's only through experience, in seeing many Toy Fox Terrier puppies, that you'll be able to make valid comparisons. The size of bone can be an indicator. A puppy with an abundance of bone, may well mature into a larger dog. This is not a foolproof clue, however, for you will occasionally encounter a large boned puppy who matures within the standard. You can also get an indication from examining the shape and size of the puppy's head. Those puppies with better shaped heads are apt to mature at a medium to large size. A puppy who has a shorter nose and a domed skull will probably be small at maturity. Eyes that have a bulgy appearance are most likely to occur on TFTs that will be small when mature. Ears can also be an indicator. Generally, the pups who will be smaller, when mature, bring their ears up first.

While none of these methods is foolproof, they will help you to "guesstimate" the size your TFT puppy will reach. Size is a complicated issue. As we've seen, it can be very difficult both to predict ultimate size and to establish consistency within your breeding program. Nothing is more frustrating than keeping a promising puppy, only to have it mature outside the limits of the standard. Still, with vigilance, selection and a measure of luck, we can make progress. Breeders must remember that Toy is an integral part of the Toy Fox Terrier's name.

6

Selecting a TFT

Buying your first Toy Fox Terrier is exciting. You've probably met a TFT owned by someone else and can't wait to have one of your own. It's better to slow down, however, and give some hard thought to your purchase. After all, the Toy Fox Terrier is a long lived breed and this dog will be with you for many years. It's best not to dash out and buy the first cute puppy you see. The more that you learn about the breed, the better your chance of finding a dog that will suit your needs and provide you with years of companionship and joy.

WHAT DO YOU WANT?

What part will the dog play in your life? Are you looking for a pet that will be a wonderful companion? Many TFTs come to be regarded as "one of the family." Do you have children in your home? Perhaps you are buying a Toy Fox Terrier that will serve primarily as your children's companion. Have you always dreamed of having a show dog? Dog showing is a wonderful hobby and, of course, it's more fun to win than lose. Will you want to breed your dog? If so, size and quality will be a consideration. You won't want to buy a dog with a serious fault if you plan on eventually breeding. All of these things will have to be taken into consideration.

A responsible breeder can be a great help to you in locating just the right dog. In order for him to do this, however, you'll have to be honest with him. Tell the breeder what you want. Remember, the breeder has invested time, effort and money in his dogs. His concern for them extends far beyond the money he will receive. No breeder wants to hear complaints and no buyer wants to be disappointed with his purchase. With cooperation, both of you can be satisfied. You'll have the dog that suits you and fulfills your needs, and the breeder will know that his dog has found a loving home.

WHERE TO BUY

Where can you locate a breeder of Toy Fox Terriers? There are a variety of ways to find a breeder. By perusing your local newspaper, you may be able to locate a nearby breeder. You can also contact the United Kennel Club or one of the many Toy Fox Terrier clubs (see the appendix for addresses). The U.K.C. will be glad to provide you with a list of Toy Fox Terrier breeders.

Ch. "PR" Cheetham's Samantha of Brookside, as a puppy, plays with her grandsire, Ch. "PR" Cheetham's Parky of Brookside. Samantha was bred by Hal and Helene Cheetham, and owned by Hopkins Kennel.

If you're looking for a dog for breeding or show, you should definitely subscribe to the UKC's publication, *Bloodlines.* You'll find information on shows, articles concerning TFTs and, of course, advertisements from serious breeders. If there's a show in your area, by all means, plan to attend. You will have the opportunity to see dogs from a variety of kennels and will be able to determine what you like. Other dog magazines may be helpful, too. They sometimes contain advertisements for Toy Fox Terriers. The bulk of TFT advertising, however, is carried in *Bloodlines.*

Toy Fox Terriers are occasionally seen in pet shops. Generally, it's best to steer clear of pet shop puppies. Since most reputable breeders refuse to sell puppies to pet shops, you're likely to pay a high price for a poor quality pup. In addition, the pet shop will be able to provide you with only sketchy information on the breed. You're far better off dealing with a breeder who knows the TFT and is committed to the breed. If a problem should arise, the breeder will be there to assist you.

If you are fortunate enough to locate a breeder in your area, definitely make an appointment to visit his home or kennel. Do your own overall evaluation. Is the kennel clean? Do the dogs look well cared for? If you plan to breed your TFT, look carefully at the size of dogs housed in the kennel. If there are a large number of oversize or extremely small TFTs, you might want to look elsewhere. Watch the breeder and see how he relates to his dogs. Look for a breeder who is knowledgeable, takes pride in his dogs, and obviously loves them.

50

TFTS AND CHILDREN

Dogs and children have a unique rapport. In fact, owning a pet can be a very special experience for a child. A dog can provide a youngster with unconditional love and a deep sense of friendship. Psychologists have recently discovered that dogs and children develop especially close bonds. By using dogs, they have managed to reach many emotionally disturbed and withdrawn children. Dogs also aid in developing the growing child's character. By caring for and training the dog, children learn responsibility. The dog/child bond also helps to instill a sense of understanding, kindness and compassion.

Many Toy Fox Terriers prove to be fantastic children's companions. As a toy dog, however, the TFT is not suited to all children. While the TFT is a hardy little dog, he is prone to broken legs and cannot tolerate excessively rough handling. The decision to purchase a TFT for your child must be based on your assessment of the child's personality and behavior. A sedate child will learn to handle even the smallest TFT with tenderness. A more active youngster may find the perfect companion in a larger TFT. For the heavy handed toddler, who's likely to hit or engage in ear pulling, a larger breed would be more appropriate.

A kindergarten student learns the proper way to handle a TFT, with the assistance of Ch. "PR" Bay Toys Monkey Shine, owned by Loren and Shirley Stroud, of Victoria, Texas.

No matter what size TFT is best for your child, there are some factors that must be borne in mind. No matter how desperately the child wants a Toy Fox Terrier, parents must remember that dog ownership is a family venture. As a parent, you have ultimate responsibility for the dog. You must teach the child how to care for and handle the dog properly. If the child forgets to feed the dog, then you must willingly step in. You must be prepared to care for the dog without resentment. If you don't want the dog every bit as much as your child does, then don't make the purchase.

PURCHASING A PET

While most breeders hope to have a whole litter of show quality puppies, this rarely happens. It's far more likely that there will be pups in each litter who lack some fine point required for success in the show ring.

Such "pet quality" puppies are usually available at a lower price. This can be a boon for the person seeking a companion. While the puppy may not have what it takes to be a show winner, he still comes from the same stock as his more illustrious brethren. He's been reared in the same way and received an identical amount of love and care.

Just because your puppy is labelled as pet quality and costs less, this does not mean that he's inferior. Indeed, the difference between a show and pet quality puppy may not be outwardly discernible. A puppy with a slight underbite may appear to be equal or superior to his champion brother. This fault, however, will prohibit him from winning in the ring, and so he is sold as a pet and should not be bred. This does not in any way impair the dog's ability to function as a wonderful companion. The pet quality dog is every bit as intelligent and loving as his show quality littermates.

In purchasing a pet, temperament will be of prime importance. By closely observing a litter, you'll see indications of future temperament. Spend some time watching the litter at play. See how they interact with people, including their breeder. Chances are you'll be able to spot the most aggressive pup, the quiet one and the one who's most attentive. You want a sensible puppy with a stable personality. Pet owners often say that their puppy "chose them." That's not a bad way to go.

SHOW AND BREEDING STOCK

A show quality puppy is one who conforms to the standard and can be

TFTs are ideal companions for the elderly as illustrated by Gr. Ch. "PR" Gordon's Maverick, owned by Olen Nichols, of Pinole, California.

A gorgeous TFT puppy. This is what you should look for in a show prospect. This little charmer, "PR" Country Toy's Shane, is owned by Joni Blaha, of Wapakoneta, Ohio.

expected to win in the show ring. It can be tricky to pick future show winners. The only guaranteed way to be assured of getting a show quality dog is to purchase an older dog who's already out there consistently winning. Still, if you have your heart set on a puppy, there are some points to bear in mind. Familiarize yourself with the standard, learn what you like and choose a breeder whose stock appeals to you. A breeder who's been working with his bloodline for years, and knows how his stock matures, will have a good idea which puppies will grow into superior TFTs. He will have the advantage of knowing how the puppy's ancestors matured and what they looked like at a young age.

Expect to pay more for the show quality puppy. You may also find that the show quality pup is slightly older. The breeder may well have recognized his potential and held him until a show home could be found. Since the breeder has more invested in the puppy, he'll ask a higher price.

In choosing the show quality puppy, there are certain things you'll want to see. It's obvious that the dog should not have any points listed as faults in the standard. A good head, sound legs, a strong topline, high tailset and good movement are musts. If you plan on breeding, choose a medium-sized dog. In addition, look for that "something extra." A dog which exudes that indefinable "class" will generally go far. If you are looking at a group of show quality puppies and there's one you just can't take your eyes off, pick him.

There are additional points you should keep in mind. You want your Toy Fox Terrier to be capable of producing healthy, strong puppies of good quality. Look for the dog who comes from a long line of healthy dogs. Females should descend from a line of bitches who whelp easily and freely. Ask about the percentage of oversize or undersize dogs produced from that bloodline. There will be some, but if the majority of dogs conform to the size you like, the bitch will be apt to produce that size. Finally, look for the names of males and females, in the pedigree, who have a reputation for producing top quality offspring. If your TFT comes from a long line of males and females who've produced champions, he's most likely to continue the tradition.

PAPERS AND REGISTRATION

Make sure that you receive the United Kennel Club registration papers

53

when you purchase your dog. It's best to select your dog from a "PR" bred litter. In the 1930's, the U.K.C. registered the "PR," or "Purple Ribbon" designation with the United States Department of Commerce. Dogs with six generations of known ancestors, three generations of which are registered with the U.K.C., earn "PR" status.

The back of the Registration Certificate, or the "Bill of Sale," should be filled out at the time of purchase. The seller will fill in the date, his city, state and zip code and sign the form. You should fill in your name, address and phone number and affix your signature. If you wish to change the dog's name, now is the time. If you're dealing with an out of town breeder, who will be shipping the dog to you, he will probably fill in the Bill of Sale for you. Be sure to sign your name and send the form to the U.K.C.. A knowledgeable breeder will be glad to answer your questions about U.K.C. procedures. If you have any other questions, contact the U.K.C..

SELECTING A HEALTHY PUPPY

Of course, you want to select a healthy puppy. Even though you aren't a veterinarian, there are some indicators you can check. Look for an overall healthy appearance. The pup's eyes should be clear and bright, not runny. His coat should be shiny and free of any rough patches or bald spots. Lift up the lip and look at the gums. They should be bright pink. Avoid the puppy with white gums, as he may have a severe case of worms. Watch the puppies play and see if they appear frisky and alert. These are good overall indicators of health.

Ask the breeder to write out the dates when the puppy received its shots. If he gave the vaccinations himself, ask for the type of vaccine used. The breeder should also tell you when the next shots are due. Most reputable breeders will allow you to take the puppy to a veterinarian for examination. Ask how long you have to take the puppy to the vet. Most breeders will allow you 24 hours. If it's a weekend, of course, extra time should be granted. Make certain that the breeder will return your money or allow you to select another animal if the dog fails the vet's examination.

Ask the breeder how often the dog is fed and what feed he's been using. Even if you intend to change the dog's feed, it's best to keep him on the diet he's accustomed to for the first few days. You can then introduce the new food gradually, by mixing it with his current diet. This will help to eliminate digestive upsets. It's also a good idea to find out when the dog had his last meal. Stop by the grocery store and pick up the food recommended by the breeder. If you're by yourself and you hesitate to leave the puppy alone in the car, ask the breeder for enough food for the next feeding. If you are purchasing the dog on a weekend and fear that you won't be able to locate the appropriate food, offer to pay the breeder for several days supply.

Now that you finally have your Toy Fox Terrier puppy, take him home and enjoy him. He'll soon worm his way into your heart and you won't be able to imagine how you got along without him. You'll quickly discover why owners become sold on this breed.

7

Caring for Your TFT

Toy Fox Terriers are animated, bouncy dogs with extraordinary energy packed into a compact frame. If we could bottle even a small percentage of the breed's abundant energy for resale, we'd all be rich. We are indeed fortunate that our breed is blessed with good health. While problems can occur in individual dogs, of course, there are no widespread health or genetic problems associated with the TFT. Since these little dogs become important family members, we are also fortunate that they are so long lived. I've heard of a Toy Fox Terrier that lived past twenty years of age. TFTs who live fifteen to eighteen years are not uncommon and one frequently hears of dogs who reach thirteen years of age. To insure that your Toy Fox Terrier lives a happy, healthy, full life, you, his owner, need to care for him sensibly. With proper care, you'll be able to enjoy the companionship of your TFT for many, many years.

SETTING THE RIGHT TONE

If your Toy Fox Terrier is to become a pleasurable companion, it's necessary to establish the right tone in your relationship from the very beginning. TFTs, particularly young puppies, are adorable. Beneath that cute exterior, however, can lie the heart of a tyrant. Even the smallest puppy can be amazingly willful. Owners of toy dogs are often apt to give in to their demanding youngster. After all, if he doesn't want to walk on a leash, why should he? It's so much easier to just scoop him up and tuck him under your arm. You may think it's amusing to watch your TFT puppy growl and attack someone's pants leg. When he's full grown and the person he attacks is your elderly, frail grandmother, it's going to seem less charming. From the very beginning, strive for a well mannered and well trained dog. It's possible to be kind, generous and loving with your dog, without being indulgent and spoiling him unnecessarily.

To achieve this, it's best to decide that you will discipline your pup from the day you get him. Your TFT must know that you love him and you will be kind to him. However, he should also know that you are the boss and when you give an order it is not to be ignored. You'll be perfectly happy to lavish him with affection, but only when he pleases you and acts correctly. You will not tolerate a dog that's "spoiled rotten." Be patient, be firm and be consistent. Your dog will come to understand what's expected of him.

WHERE WILL YOUR TFT SLEEP?

The grown TFT will generally select his own spot for sleeping. It may be a favorite chair, a warm spot by the fireplace or he may want to share your bed. For the puppy, however, you should provide a bed of some kind. This is best until your TFT is fully housebroken and can be trusted. There are a variety of dog beds on the market and they range from the simple to the elaborate. It's best to avoid wooden or wicker beds for the young puppy, however. Puppies have a tendency to chew on these materials while teething. Metal beds, with foam rubber mattresses, covered in a washable fabric are quite practical. You may want to purchase a dog crate, such as the ones used by the airlines for shipping dogs. This will allow your dog to have his own private place, where he can feel secure and safe. The crate will come in handy if you plan on taking your dog to shows or traveling with him. If you're short on money, however, a puppy bed need not be elaborate. A large, heavy cardboard box makes a suitable bed. These can often be obtained free of charge at grocery or appliance stores.

Given a chance, most TFTs would prefer to share your bed with you. After all, you consider it nice and comfy, and there's nothing your dog likes better than being close to you. If you want your little dog to sleep on your bed, that's fine. It's important to remember, however, that once you allow the dog to sleep with you, it will be very difficult to reverse the practice. It's best to let your puppy grow up before you allow him to sleep on the bed. Toy Fox Terriers have brittle bones. Young puppies are, particularly, vulnerable. It's very easy to break those little legs and a bad spill can even result in a broken neck.

Jumping on and off beds, or inadvertently falling from them, can represent a very real danger. It's best to let your puppy grow up and learn to judge heights before allowing him to share your bed. If you do give in and allow the dog access to your bed, you may want to provide him with a little footstool or other platform. Place the stool at the foot or side of the bed. This way, your

Proper diet, veterinary care and grooming will produce a beautifully conditioned TFT. Gr. Ch. "PR" Toy Gems Toy Maker, owned by Herb Neider, of Chesapeake, Virginia, radiates health and vitality.

TFT will have an intermediate step to aid him in reaching the bed.

FEEDING YOUR TFT

Dog owners today are truly blessed to have at their fingertips an amazing array of scientifically balanced dog foods. You may chose to feed your Toy Fox Terrier a dry dog meal, a canned food or a semi-moist feed. No matter which kind of food you select, you should examine the label to make sure that it's "nutritionally complete." This will insure that your dog gets the proper blend of protein, fats, vitamins and minerals.

Toy Fox Terriers thrive on a variety of diets. As a rule, dogs of this breed are good eaters. Over the years, most breeders have experimented and determined the diet that best suits their dogs. Ideas about the proper diet for a TFT vary. This simply illustrates that there is more than one way to feed a Toy Fox Terrier and still maintain his condition. Unlike people, most dogs thrive on monotony. They are creatures of habit. Once you find a food that is palatable to your dog, it's best to stick with that food, rather than continuously switching brands. Encourage your dog to develop good feeding habits. Ideally, he should eat his food within minutes of your setting it out for him.

As I've said, each breeder will eventually arrive at a diet his dogs are comfortable with. At Hopkins' Toy Fox Terrier Kennels, this is the diet that I use. For my adult dogs (excluding pregnant females), I feed an equal mixture of Purina Dog Chow and Purina Hi-Protein meal. I moisten the meal with hot water and allow it to stand until the food has softened. Most of my dogs receive one to one-and-a-half cups per day. I also purchase a powdered milk, intended for use in raising baby calves. I combine one cup of this milk powder with two quarts of lukewarm water. Each adult dog receives one-third to one-half cup of milk following their regular feeding. I know that some breeders have experienced stomach upsets in giving their dogs milk or milk products. This has not proven to be a problem in my kennel. Active studs, older females and dogs I'm actively showing, are given an additional meat supplement. For this, I prefer a mixture of canned chicken meat and a semi-moist food, such as Gaines Top Choice, Puppy Choice or Purina Moist and Meaty. I mix one packet of the semi-moist food with one can of the chicken meat. A spoonful or two of this is mixed with the regular feed.

Breeders are often asked how many times a day a Toy Fox Terrier should be fed. Growing puppies need twice as many calories as an adult dog. Depending on the puppy's age, he may require two to four feedings a day. It's best to check with the breeder, or your veterinarian, and follow their recommendations. Adult dogs need only one or two meals per day. I feed my dogs only once daily, but I do know that some breeders prefer to feed two smaller meals per day. Most dogs appreciate regularity. It's best to feed them at approximately the same time every day. This is one of the best ways to instill good eating habits.

Be sure to provide your dog with plenty of fresh, clean water. Ideally, he should have water available to him whenever he's awake. It's best to avoid allowing your dog to drink too much cold water after a hard play period. Give him a small drink, and when he's quieted down, offer more.

HOUSEBREAKING YOUR TFT

Most owners prefer to train their dogs, from an early age, to eliminate outside in the yard. Apartment owners, however, sometimes prefer to have their dogs paper trained. It is possible, with a toy breed like the TFT, to depend entirely on paper training. For others, paper training may be an interim measure. If a puppy was purchased during winter, and the harsh weather makes it unsuitable to take him outside, paper training may be employed until the weather improves. Whichever method you use, you'll want to begin housebreaking as soon as you bring your new dog home.

One of the important factors in housebreaking a puppy is vigilance. You want to catch the puppy before he has an accident. If you note your dog beginning to squat, say "No" in a harsh voice. This will usually stop him momentarily. It will enable you to pick him up and place him on the paper or carry him to the yard. If the puppy has an accident and you're right there, scold him. Take him immediately to his paper or the yard so that he learns to understand this is what you want. If you discover that he's had a previous accident, just quietly clean it up. It will do no good to castigate him for an accident made an hour before. Hitting the dog with a rolled up newspaper is, likewise, not very effective. When the dog does his duty, either on the papers or in the yard, praise him profusely. You may feel stupid praising a dog for going to the bathroom, but it is beneficial. Your compliments of "good dog" will get the message across.

While housebreaking your dog, it's best to restrict his range within the house. Confine him to the kitchen, for instance, if you can't supervise his movements. If he is loose in the house, make certain to keep an eye on him at all times. That way, you'll be able to intervene if he starts to have an accident. Watch your dog closely and learn his habits. Many dogs will sniff the floor or turn in circles before they begin to eliminate. This can serve as a good warning for you. Tell the dog, "No," scoop him under your arm and carry him outdoors or to his paper.

There will be certain times when your dog is most likely to relieve himself. You should take him out first thing in the morning and last thing at night. You'll also want to take him outside or to the paper after each meal or after he's been drinking water. Dogs are often most prone to relieve themselves after a play period. By taking your dog out at these critical times, you'll avoid most accidents.

If you are paper training your TFT, begin by spreading newspapers over a large area of the floor. Try to determine precisely where you want the papers to lie. You don't want to continually move them and confuse the dog. If, for some reason, you find it necessary to shift the papers to a different location, do this gradually. Day by day, slide the papers closer to the desired spot. All papers containing bowel movements, should be removed as soon as possible. It's often beneficial, however, to leave a paper spotted with urine. This will entice the dog to return to the spot. Gradually, as your dog consistently uses the papers, you can remove some of them. You'll no longer need to cover such a wide area.

Housebreaking a dog can, at times, prove frustrating. However, Toy Fox Terriers are naturally clean dogs. Most TFTs will learn what's expected of them in short order. Some dogs will be housebroken in a matter of days. Occasionally, one will run across a dog who takes weeks to become trustworthy. Don't despair and don't become discouraged. Screaming and yelling will only make the whole situation more tense. Just follow the rules outlined above and stick by them.

LEASH BREAKING

You'll want to leash, or lead, break your Toy Fox Terrier. Some people who buy toy dogs, make the mistake of not lead breaking them. They find it easier to just tuck the dog under their arm when they go out. However, there are times when having a leash broken dog is a great convenience. It's safer for your little dog to be on a leash and you'll be able to maintain better control of him. There will also be times when you want your hands free. Of course, if you plan to show your Toy Fox Terrier, leash breaking is a must.

Most Toy Fox Terriers are easy to leash break. Occasionally, however, one can get a stubborn dog who objects to having anything around his neck. This type of dog can be trained. It will just take a little longer and require more patience. Your dog may be fully lead broken after only one session. A headstrong dog may require a week or more of work.

It's advisable to introduce your TFT to the leash gradually. A lightweight, one piece show lead is best for leash breaking. Place the leash around your dog's neck. Call his name and talk excitedly to him. Try walking him back and forth. Talk to him all the while, telling him how good he is. You may want to snap your fingers or make little clicking noises. You'll soon learn what is best for keeping your dog's attention. Remember, you must make this fun. If your dog follows you, praise him enthusiastically. Repeat this for a few minutes each day for the next week.

Your TFT should be prohibited from jumping on and off furniture during puppyhood. Here is "PR" Five Oaks Brother John, owned by Chet and Kathleen Cornwell, of Aripeka, Florida, with his leg in a cast.

59

TFTs will accept other dogs if raised with them. These fine TFTs are owned by Ruth Siptroth, of E. Stroudsburg, Pennsylvania.

If your dog objects to walking on the leash, you'll have to take the training a little more slowly. Sit down on the floor with your dog. Place the leash on him and spend a few minutes playing with him. Try letting him run around with the leash on. Be sure to keep a close eye on him. You don't want him to get wrapped around the leg of a chair or caught on something. Pick up the end of the lead. Follow the puppy around, holding the lead, while he explores. Stop and encourage the dog to come to you. If he refuses, kneel down and tap your fingers on the floor. This will usually attract his attention and get him to come. Should he still refuse, very gently pull him to you. Once he gets to you, pick him up, cuddle him and tell him how wonderful he is for responding. Now, try walking again. If your dog should balk, you'll have to begin all over again. Some headstrong dogs will firmly plant their feet and refuse to move. One occasionally encounters a dog who leaps about like a bucking bronco. He spins in the air and won't keep all four feet on the ground. For this type of dog, persistence is the answer. Just keep giving him short sessions where you make it clear that you expect him to walk. Sooner or later, he will realize that you aren't going to give up.

GROOMING YOUR TFT

The TFT requires only minimal grooming. In fact, this is one of the great advantages of Toy Fox Terrier ownership. This does not mean, however, that grooming is unimportant. Your dog will look and feel better if he's groomed regularly. A dog who is well fed, well cared for and has adequate exercise will usually have a shining, healthy coat. External parasites, such as fleas, can cause the coat to become dry and brittle. Internal parasites (worms) can also wreak havoc with the TFT's coat. Likewise, a dog who is fed a poor diet, particularly one deficient in fat, may have a dry coat. By paying close attention to these factors, however, your TFT's coat will remain lustrous and satiny.

Regular weekly grooming will keep your Toy Fox Terrier looking his best. Frequent grooming will also help to eliminate any "doggy" odor. Weekly grooming should consist of a thorough brushing with a soft-bristled brush. Begin at the neck and work your way to the tail. If you like, you can follow the brushing with a finger massage. This will help to keep your TFT's skin supple.

You'll also want to inspect your dog's ears when grooming him. Fortunately, with their upright ears, TFTs rarely have ear problems. The inside of the ear can become dirty, though. Clean the ears with a cotton ball or swab. You may wish to moisten the swab with a little alcohol. Under no circumstances should you probe deeper than the eye can see. Regular inspection of the feet is also beneficial. Look for any sore spots or cracks in the pads. These should be treated promptly.

Toy Fox Terriers frequently experience dental problems but, with frequent cleaning, you can help to avoid these difficulties. There are a number of concoctions you can use to clean your dog's teeth. In her excellent book, *Dogs and How to Groom Them,* Hilary Harmar makes several suggestions. "A solution of half and half cold milk and peroxide vol. 10 is excellent for cleaning the teeth, as is a mixture of salt and baking soda moistened sufficiently to form a paste, or even human toothpaste. Dogs do not care for the teeth cleaning operation. It is therefore important to do it gently, quickly, yet thoroughly, and to give great praise afterward." Cleaning your dog's teeth regularly will do much to eliminate the build up of tartar. If your TFT does have a heavy tartar accumulation, you may have to take more drastic measures. Purchase a metal tooth scaler. These are available from many dog supply houses. When scaling teeth, try not to scrape too vigorously. You want to remove the tartar, but you don't want to chip the coat of enamel covering each tooth.

On a monthly basis, you'll want to clip your dog's nails. Some dogs, particularly those kept on rough surfaces, will wear their nails down naturally. Most dogs, however, will need their nails clipped periodically. It's important to keep your dogs' nails cut back. Nails which are allowed to grow long will cause the feet to splay. Most breeders use a guillotine type clipper. Some dogs strongly object to having their nails clipped, and you may want an assistant to help you. It's also sometimes beneficial to shield the dog's eyes so he doesn't see the actual clipping. Try your best to determine exactly where the quick (vein) in the nail ends. This vein is easily seen in dogs with light colored nails. For the dark nailed dog, you'll want to take off only the tip of the nail. Place the nail clipper over the nail and snip the tip off rapidly in a single cut. If you should, accidentally, cut into the vein, just apply a little styptic powder. Each time you cut your dog's nails, the vein will recede slightly. Therefore, the more often you clip the dog's nails, the shorter they can be kept.

Toy Fox Terriers rarely need to be bathed. In fact, frequent bathing is not good for the TFT coat, as it removes the hair's natural oils. There are some instances, though, when baths are a must. If your TFT has just wallowed in a mud puddle, rolled on something disgusting, or if you're readying him for a show, then a bath is in order. Bathing is essentially the same as for any other dog. Due to the TFT's small size, however, he can generally be bathed in the kitchen sink. Do be sure, however, to close the windows. You must protect the dog from drafts until he's completely dry. There are a vast array of dog shampoos on the market, and most will work quite well on your dog. If fleas are a problem in your area, look for a shampoo which kills them. Be sure to carefully clean the dog's bedding to prevent further infestation.

YOUR TFT'S HEALTH

Your TFT will need periodic veterinary visits to safeguard his health. Routine vaccinations will help to protect him. All dogs should be vaccinated, on a yearly basis, for distemper, hepatitis, leptospirosis and parvovirus. You may also wish to have your dog immunized to prevent kennel cough, or parainfluenza. Check with your veterinarian to determine if there are any diseases prevalent in your region and if a vaccine is available to protect your dog. Thanks to modern vaccines, many highly contagious diseases are almost a thing of the past. Your Toy Fox Terrier will also need a rabies vaccination. Check with your vet to determine how often this should be given. Some states require yearly inoculations while others stipulate that vaccination should be given once every three years.

It's a good idea to take your dog to a veterinarian once or twice a year for a general routine examination. Such periodic check-ups will help to detect any problems, before they become serious. Take along a stool sample so your vet can examine it microscopically for worms. If your vet finds evidence of worms, he can supply you with the appropriate medication. Ask your veterinarian if heartworm is prevalent in your area. A simple preventative medication, given daily or monthly, will prevent infestation.

By feeding your TFT properly, caring for his health and grooming him regularly, you'll insure that he stays in prime condition. Consistent training and discipline will help him to become an ideal companion. Be sure not to forget the most important ingredient of all...LOVE, and lots of it! Toy Fox Terriers thrive on love and attention. By building a close rapport with your dog, he'll become your true friend.

8

The Stud Dog

Great care should be taken in the selection of a stud dog. Whether you are purchasing a male for your own use or planning to pay a fee for the use of an outside dog, much thought should go into the choice. The male Toy Fox Terrier can have a tremendous impact on the breed. While a female will have only one, or at most two litters a year, a male can be bred many, many times. He can pass on his good qualities, as well as his faults, to a great number of offspring. Indeed, a very popular stud, used for many years, can have a far-reaching impact on the breed.

What should you look for in a stud dog? Just because a male is a registered purebred, he is not automatically qualified to be a stud. Even those interested only in breeding pets should still be guided by the standard and attempt to produce typical Toy Fox Terriers. A male intended for stud usage should be a good representative of the breed. While he needn't be a champion, he should, nevertheless, excel in the basic breed virtues and have no glaring faults. A Toy Fox Terrier who has a poor bite, lop ears, a sway back, cowhocks, a poor front or unacceptable color should not be used for breeding. An oversize dog would also be a poor candidate for stud use.

You'll want to make sure that the male has both testicles. A cryptorchid male, or one with no testicles, will be sterile. A monorchid male (one with only a single testicle descended), however, may well be fertile. Monorchidism is a disqualification in the breed ring and, since the condition may well be hereditary, you should avoid the stud with only one testicle.

Pedigree is of great importance when you're deciding on a stud. The pedigree should reflect a background of careful breeding. Since the stud dog passes on the qualities transmitted to him by his ancestors, it will help if you can learn as much as possible about the dogs named in the pedigree. Look for a balanced breeding, with good dogs on both sides of the stud's pedigree. It may be tempting to use a dog sired by "Grand Champion 'PR' Mr. Wonderful," but if his mother was "'PR' Little Miss I have Every Fault" then you are just as likely to get puppies resembling the grandmother as you are Mr. Wonderful.

The real "proof of the pudding," with a stud dog, is how well he can produce. The effectiveness of a stud dog should be measured by the quality of his progeny. It's a sad fact of life that some spectacular show winners never sire progeny as good as themselves. Conversely, some less flashy dog may consistently produce outstanding offspring. If you are using an outside stud, try to obtain as much information as possible about the quality of the Toy Fox

Terriers he has produced. If you are using one of your own studs, keep detailed records and photos of his offspring. Check back with puppy buyers and try to see (in person or in photos) how the puppies matured. This way you will be able to see if your dog is living up to his potential as a stud.

While physical qualities are undeniably important, don't forget to look for a dog that excels in temperament. A dog passes on not only his conformation, but also his mental characteristics. A TFT who is shy and sluggish or overly aggressive is not typical and makes an unsuitable stud dog. You must remember that the majority of your puppies will probably enter pet homes, where temperament will be of prime importance.

Gr. Ch. "PR" Park's Rudy of Brookside, owned by W. H. and Mary Parks, of Tulsa, Oklahoma, is the sire of Champions and Grand Champions.

Last, but certainly not least, you want a dog who is healthy and vigorous. It's best if he comes from a background of long-lived, healthy dogs. You also want a dog who is a reliable breeder. While a dog's reliability as a stud is often molded by his early breeding experiences, the dog that is uniformly healthy and hardy is most likely to consistently have a good sperm count. Bitches bred to such a vigorous dog are more likely to become pregnant and deliver strong puppies.

All breeders hope that they will have a prepotent stud. This is a male who is dominant for his virtues and can overcome the faults of most bitches. He can be used with success on a wide variety of bitches. Such studs can quickly make a name for a kennel and contribute much to their success. You are indeed fortunate if you discover that you own such a dog. A truly prepotent male comes along rarely, so take advantage of him if you are lucky enough to own one. Don't hesitate to seek the services of a prepotent stud owned by another breeder.

RAISING THE STUD DOG

Experienced breeders have learned that healthy, hardy dogs are most likely to be active, vigorous studs. A good, well-balanced diet, coupled with plenty of exercise, is important for the stud dog. You want him in top-notch condition. Be sure to check for both internal and external parasites. Worms and fleas will sap his energy, and a male in run down condition may well have a below normal sperm count.

"PR" DeBurger's Buster"s Buddy

Ch. "PR" Currens' Daniboy of Parkside

"PR" DeBurger's Cutie Pie

Ch. Currens' Tally of Parkside

Ch. "PR" Currens' Billy Gay of Parkside

Ch. "PR" Currens' Gena of Parkside

"PR" Hopkins' Inky

Ch. "PR" Curren's Parkside Deuce

"PR" McKenzie's Mr. Vick

Ch. "PR" Senfts' Sir Rebel

"PR" McKenzie's Judy

Ch. "PR" Currens' Viva of Parkside

"PR" Miller's Mr. Doby

Ch. "PR" Senfts' Cindy Lou Gay

"PR" Miller's Jody

Ch. "PR" Hopkins' Gay Danny
Born: Dec. 15, 1977

Ch. "PR" Cheetham's Gay Jet of Brookside

Ch. "PR" Cheetham's Cyclone of Brookside

Ch. "PR" Cheetham's Raineey of Brookside

Ch. "PR" Hopkins' Barnstormer

Ch. "PR" Yancey's Rinebold Skipper

Ch. "PR" Hopkins' Sara Ann

"PR" Hopkins' Helene

Ch. "PR" Hopkiins' Gay Tammy

Ch. "PR" Currens' Billy Gay of Parkside

Ch. "PR" Hopkins' Andy Gay

"PR" Shumaker's Ima-Dandy

Ch. "PR" Hopkins' Gay Gem

"PR" Steiner's Gay China Boy

Ch. "PR" Hopkins' Tammy's Little Jewel

Ch. "PR" Nethery's Miss Tammy

*A four generation pedigree of Danny,
the first champion of the breed with a
three generation, all champion pedigree.*

The mental attitude of a stud dog is important. You want a lively, confident dog, who is sure of himself and enthusiastic about breeding. Therefore, he must be handled differently than a pet male. At an early age, your male dog will begin to mount and ride other dogs. Do not be upset if you find him trying to mount other males. He may even latch on to your leg and thrust enthusiastically. While it would be acceptable to chastise a pet male, you'll have to be more inventive with the future stud dog. Repeatedly telling him "No," at an early age, may discourage him. You don't want to convey the impression that breeding is wrong. If he becomes too much of a nuisance, separate him from the other dogs. If he's riding your leg, you might try distracting his attention with a favorite toy, or take him out for a walk.

If at all possible, you'll want to breed your dog for the first time while he's still young. Many breeders find eight to ten months an ideal age to begin. All TFTs are individuals, though, and an occasional male will take longer to become interested in breeding. Once a male has sired his first litter, he is referred to as a "proven" stud.

That first breeding is very important. You want everything to go well, as this experience will set the tone for future breedings. Take the time to observe your dog's actions closely. You will see how he responds to females in season and how he approaches the mating process. You will also be training your dog to be the type of stud you want. He will learn to respond to your encouragement, you'll aid him by holding the bitch so that he can breed her successfully and efficiently, and you will both learn to function together as a team. While it will take time and patience to accomplish this, you will find that the time is well spent, as you will end up with the type of reliable and eager stud you can always count on.

It's best if your dog's first breeding is to a proven, easily bred bitch. Working with two inexperienced dogs can try the patience of the most experienced breeder. The maiden bitch is likely to flirt and to sit down when the male tries to mount her. Even worse, she may snap at him as he mounts. While some dogs will ignore this, it could confuse and discourage your inexperienced male, and spoil his enthusiasm for breeding. If you have little experience yourself and you must breed two unproven dogs, then it might be wise to obtain the help of an experienced breeder.

The inexperienced male is more apt to flirt and play with the female. Some of this should be permitted for it will increase his excitement. However, you don't want him to get into the habit of playing excessively. You want him to attend to the business at hand. Verbally encourage him. You don't want to talk so much that you distract him, but you do want to let him know that you approve of what he's doing. No matter how frustrated you become, don't lose your patience. This could ruin the dog for future breedings. Take your time and don't hurry him. He'll soon have the idea.

Some breeders simply put the male and female in a run and leave them alone for several days hoping that they will breed. This is an inefficient and dangerous way of handling breeding. They have no idea if or precisely when

Gr. Ch. "PR" Hopkins' Hi-Anthony, poses proudly with his trophies. This 6 pound dog is owned by Joni Blaha, of Wapakoneta, Ohio.

the female was bred. This makes it difficult to plan for the whelping. If you are controlling the breeding and for some reason the stud will not service the bitch, all is not lost. You may still have time to try another stud with the bitch. Also, accidents do occasionally happen and either the bitch or, more likely, the stud could be injured. By controlling the breeding you will be able to avoid a calamity.

It's best to teach your stud dog that you will hold the bitch for him. Some males, particularly those who've bred on their own for the first time, will have nothing to do with a female if you insist on holding her. This can lead to problems when you try him with a difficult bitch. If you are breeding a small stud to a larger female, you may have to reposition the dogs so they can breed successfully. A male who will not allow you to assist will be annoying. Encourage the stud to mount the bitch while you hold her. Beware of talking too much when he's attempting to actually penetrate her. After he's tied, you may indeed pet him and tell him how pleased you are with the job he's done. This way he will learn to be comfortable with having you touch him during the breeding process.

A good stud can continue to sire puppies into his old age. After the age of eight to ten years, however, you may note that some of the bitches he has bred do not conceive. His fertility may diminish during hot weather, for instance. If you're not ready to permanently retire your still valuable stud, you may wish to arrange for periodic sperm counts to be taken.

You may want to allow the dogs to become familiar before the breeding. Some owners place the dogs in adjacent runs so that they can become acquainted with each other. In larger breeds, it often takes two people to handle the breeding. With the small Toy Fox Terrier, however, it's possible for one person to control both the dog and the bitch. If you are uncertain, placing a leash on the bitch will give you added control.

Take a few moments to plan for the breeding, before you bring out both dogs. You'll want to do the breeding in a small area where the dogs will be free from distraction. It's best if the stud is familiar with the area, so that he will feel comfortable. You want a surface where your male will have good footing. If you'll be breeding the dogs in the house, you may want to spread out a piece of old carpeting. Be aware that there may be a few dribbles and be sure to protect your regular carpet. If your stud is smaller than the bitch, you might want to have a small rug on hand. This can be folded so that he can stand on it and elevate his height.

Be sure to prepare for your own comfort, too. Once the male penetrates the female, his penis will swell and the dogs will become "tied" together. A tie may last only a few minutes or it could continue for an hour. Most ties last between 15-25 minutes. Try to make yourself as comfortable as you can. If you find a position where you're able to rest your back against a wall, you may be more comfortable. You don't want to be distracted, either. If you're breeding your dogs in the house, take the telephone off the hook. If you're expecting an important phone call, try to move the telephone within reach.

If you wish you may allow the dogs to play and flirt for a few minutes. Sit down on the floor near the dogs and keep a hand on the bitch. Hold her firmly with your hand on her shoulders or gently encircling her neck. After some initial nuzzling and licking, your male will probably start licking the bitch's vulva. If she's ready to be bred, she'll raise her tail and elevate her vulva. The male will then usually mount her. You'll have to be prepared to control the bitch if she starts to snap or tries to lie down. You'll want to try to line up the bitch and the stud. If he is out of position, very gently push him away and encourage him to try again. You will most likely be able to tell when the male has penetrated by the reaction of the bitch. Just make sure she stands solidly on all four feet until he stops thrusting. Once he's stopped, look closely and make sure the dogs are properly tied. If you see the swollen bulb of the penis outside the vagina, you have an "outside tie" and you'll have to handle this somewhat differently from the normal tie. Assuming that this is a normal breeding, your stud dog will probably slide his front feet off the bitch's back. You may notice that he is anxious to turn. Gently help him bring his hind leg over the bitch's back. Both dogs will then be standing tail to tail. If, while he's turning, your male should cry out in pain, quickly bring him back to the original position. You don't want to take the chance of injuring him.

Just when you think your back will break and your legs have gone permanently to sleep, the dogs will separate. It may take you a few seconds to realize that they are no longer linked. Some breeders like to hold the bitch's hindquarters up in the air for a few seconds to avoid losing any sperm. Others consider this a waste of time.

It's best to separate the dogs. Some terrifically enthusiastic stud dogs will mount the bitch and attempt to breed again. Give the dogs some fresh water and allow them to rest. Most breeders skip a day and then breed once more on the following day.

Following the breeding, stud dog owners should keep an eye on their dogs. Most males will retract the penis into the sheath shortly after the breeding has taken place. Occasionally, however, the tip of the penis remains red and swollen and doesn't settle back properly into the sheath. This can usually be corrected by grasping the sheath and gently massaging it, by pulling and pushing, toward the end of the penis. In most cases, this will force the penis to retract. If this problem occurs, be sure to check the dog frequently to make sure that the penis remains in the sheath. On rare occasions, it will be necessary to use a lubricant on the swollen penis to get it back into the sheath.

THE OUTSIDE TIE

An outside tie occurs when the bulb, located at the rear of a dog's penis, swells outside the bitch's vagina. An outside tie is more difficult for the inexperienced breeder to handle. Nevertheless, while less desirable than an inside tie, a properly handled outside tie is often successful. Some males seem more prone to outside ties and, while they are more trouble to breed, they can and do sire puppies.

Nat. Gr. Ch. Gorden's Shamrock Lad, owned by Doug and Betty Gorden, of Crosby, Texas, is the only TFT to twice win the National title.

It's best to hold the penis behind the swollen bulb. Place your other hand on the bitch's belly and press her backwards. You can allow the stud to turn, but it's usually easier to keep the pair linked if he remains mounted. You'll want to hold the bitch and stud together as long as possible. Though the dogs may be restless, try to keep them together for at least five minutes.

THE RELUCTANT STUD

Most Toy Fox Terriers are eager and reliable studs. Sometimes, however, despite the best of training, you'll encounter a lackadaisical stud. Such males try the patience of breeders. There will be times, despite everything you try, when you simply can't achieve a successful breeding. You'll have to decide whether you want to work with this type of stud. If he's already produced outstanding puppies or is the only male to carry on your line, then it may be worth the effort.

The reluctant stud usually flirts and plays with the bitch until he's exhausted. He seems unable to concentrate on the breeding and rapidly loses interest. You'll have to devise your own methods of dealing with the reluctant stud. Your main objective will be to perk him up and excite him. You must be inventive and extra encouraging with this type of stud. Giving in to the frustration you are bound to feel, by yelling at him, will cause the reluctant male to quit.

Try short breeding sessions for the hesitant stud. If a breeding isn't accomplished in a short amount of time, stop. Let him calm down and relax. Try again in an hour or two. If he seems intent on playing and won't respond to your encouragement, there are a few things you might try. Stand up, gather the bitch into your arms and announce that you're taking her away. If he jumps around excitedly, try once again. You might well be successful. You can also try placing the female in a crate. The male will probably circle the crate, dancing about, whining and barking. The female he showed no interest in previously, now seems terribly attractive to him. If he seems truly excited, take the bitch from the crate and try again. If, however, he lies quietly down and shows no interest, you have little chance of a successful breeding.

Sometimes jealousy can be used to excite the reluctant stud. Place the male in a crate and bring out another stud. Allow him to watch as the male flirts and attempts to breed the bitch. Of course, you must pay close attention or you're likely to get a breeding you don't want! Even the most disinterested of studs, usually gets his ire up over the sight of a rival male with *his* bitch. When you feel that he's sufficiently fired up, remove the opposing male. Your stud, now eager and excited, can be released from his crate and will often consummate the breeding.

By carefully raising your male TFT and handling his first few matings carefully, you will be well on your way to owning a reliable stud dog. With encouragement and sensible guidance, your dog will quickly learn what's expected of him. From experience, you will discover how best to handle him. And, hopefully, he'll produce many champions and grand champions for you!

9

The Brood Bitch

Much of what we've said about stud dog selection, applies equally to the brood bitch. The beginning breeder will make no more important selection than the purchase of a good brood bitch. The strength of your breeding program will be based on your continuing production of good bitches. While many breeders make a grand splash with a sensational winning dog, the true breeder knows that a line of top-producing bitches is his ticket to success. Excellent brood bitches form the cornerstone of the carefully planned breeding program. If you are using outside studs and a breeding proves unsuccessful, it's relatively easy to change course. If, however, your female is unsuitable as a brood bitch, you must either begin again or be plagued with years of trying to breed up from a mediocre start. The brood bitch is the rock upon which the foundation of your kennel will rest. Selection of the appropriate brood bitch, therefore, is essential.

The brood bitch does not necessarily have to be a champion herself. It is imperative, however, that she be carefully bred and from a line that has a reputation for producing consistent quality. After reviewing the standard carefully, decide which qualities are most important to you. Select a bitch from a line which excels in those virtues. Look for a bitch who is structurally sound and one that excels in temperament. You'll be on your way to producing Toy Fox Terriers of which you can be proud.

BREEDING SIZE

If you are thinking of breeding your Toy Fox Terrier bitch, then size is an important consideration. I consider 4 1/2 to 7 pounds to be the ideal size for brood bitches. I look for sturdy bitches that aren't overly narrow in the hips and pelvis. By following these guidelines, I've been able to minimize whelping difficulties and keep Caesarian sections to a minimum.

Some owners prefer tiny Toy Fox Terriers. Such bitches, however, are not suitable for breeding. Breeding a TFT bitch of less than 4 pounds can be extremely dangerous. Most tiny bitches simply aren't as capable of delivering their puppies naturally. A Caesarian section is often necessary for these little bitches. Administering anesthesia to any dog is risky, but it's especially perilous with tiny bitches. Make no mistake about it, a Caesarian section is stressful. Think long and hard before breeding the very small TFT bitch. You could well lose both the mother and her puppies.

While most Toy Fox Terrier bitches whelp easily and naturally, some do require Caesarians. Normal size females may require a C-section, as most breeders call them, under certain conditions. Generally this occurs when there is an overly large puppy, a dead puppy or a puppy that's mispresented. Problem puppies such as these can block the birth canal. Many bitches who, because of these problems, require C-sections can go on

This impressive female would make an ideal foundation for any kennel. Gr. Ch. "PR" McGuire's Mi-Kookie is owned by Elaine McGuire, of Melvin, Michigan.

to whelp later litters naturally.

Controversy abounds over whether bitches which routinely require Caesarians should be included in a breeding program. No breeder really likes C-sections. They're expensive, stressful to both the mother and the pups, and very inconvenient. For some perverse reason, it seems that bitches requiring Caesarians never go into labor until two or three in the morning.

Each breeder will have to decide whether it's worth including bitches requiring routine Caesarians in their breeding program. Much, of course, will depend on the quality of the bitch. If she's already produced a litter of outstanding quality, you'll doubtless grant her more latitude. If the C-section was due to an overly large puppy, a dead pup, or a difficult presentation, I will try breeding the bitch again. If the bitch requires successive Caesarians, you must decide if it's worth continuing to breed her. Some breeders accept C-sections as a way of life and anticipate them. Other breeders feel that the best way to insure a line of free-whelping bitches is to eliminate those requiring Caesarian sections from their breeding program. Regardless of quality, they don't breed C-section bitches.

Breeders are often faced with the dilemma of whether to breed oversized (larger than 7 pound) bitches. It's always a temptation, as these larger bitches may be of excellent type, often produce larger litters, and usually whelp freely. Many owners of large bitches try to mitigate the problem by breeding to tiny studs. What they don't realize is that the puppies will still inherit the genes for size. They're likely to find in their litter a lovely oversized male and a tiny bitch. If you opt to breed a large bitch, search for a properly sized male who comes from a long line of properly sized TFTs. If you can find such a male with a history of producing moderate sized offspring, you'll be better off. Don't be tempted into thinking that the male, just because he's small, will necessarily produce small size.

BREEDING AGE

Toy Fox Terrier females generally come in season for the first time between eight and eleven months of age. The majority of bitches in my kennel begin their seasons at nine to ten months. All TFTs are individuals, however, and occasionally you'll find bitches who come into season at seven months, as well as some that wait until they're almost a year old.

Most books will tell you that bitches come into season every six months. It appears, however, that most Toy Fox Terriers haven't read these books. Most TFT females come into season every seven to eight months. I have had a few, though, that did come into season every six months. A few of my bitches come into season at nine or ten month intervals. Once in a while, I've also had a rare individual who has had only one season per year.

Your female will need time to grow and mature before being bred. She must be ready, not only physically, but also emotionally and mentally, for the task of having puppies. I suggest waiting until the second season to breed your bitch. This should allow her to mature without the stress of whelping a litter. Furthermore, many TFT bitches have an incomplete first season and will fail to conceive. Under no circumstances should any bitch, no matter how large she may be, be bred so that she'll have a litter before she's one year old.

Most breeders prefer to breed their bitches, for the first time, before they reach the age of three. Certainly bitches can and do whelp successfully, for the first time, after three. Very often, however, it's more

Ch. "PR" Currens' Suzy Jr. of Parkside was the first champion from Howard and Doris Currens' illustrious Parkside Kennels, in Port Huron, Michigan. Unfortunately, she died before producing any pups.

difficult for these older bitches to conceive. Like the very young bitch, the older maiden bitch may encounter difficulties in whelping.

Novices often ask when a bitch is too old for breeding. This is difficult to answer. Breeders frequently continue to breed their bitches into their eighth year. Much depends on the health and condition of the bitch. Frequently, older bitches are less regular in their seasons than younger bitches. You should be aware that older bitches are also more prone to complications during whelping, and a Caesarian may be necessary. Still, if you want one last litter from your fabulous brood bitch and she's still in good condition, you can try. I've had a bitch as old as eleven years of age produce a litter.

Most breeders breed their brood bitches one season, then skip the next season. This allows the bitch to recover fully and replenish her resources, in preparation for her next litter. There's nothing that grieves the dog lover quite so much as seeing a bitch bred successively season after season until she wears out. If you have a bitch, however, that comes into season every ten months or only once a year, it is permissible to breed her every season. If you feel compelled to breed your bitch on successive seasons, then do allow her to rest on her third heat cycle. Above all, let common sense be your guide. If your brood bitch has a litter of one or two puppies and raises them without difficulty, it might not be too much of a strain to breed on her next season. If, however, she's just finished raising a litter of five, you're asking a great deal to expect her to raise another litter on her next season.

CONDITIONING THE FUTURE MOM

The best time to begin conditioning the brood bitch is before she's bred. Your best bet for ensuring vigorous, strong puppies and few whelping problems, is to start with a bitch in tip-top condition. Now's the perfect time for a routine veterinary visit. A fecal examination should be done to detect the presence of worms. It's best to have your bitch treated now, before she's bred. You'll also want to be sure she's up-to-date on her yearly vaccinations. Have the vet attend promptly to any vaginal infections. Immediate treatment is in order for any skin conditions that the bitch might transmit to the puppies.

Now is also the time to stop for a moment and take a long look at the future mom's physique. You want to have her in good, hard condition. A flabby, overweight bitch may have difficulty becoming pregnant. She could also encounter whelping difficulties. Place her on a diet before you breed her. Similarly, the thin, underweight bitch is apt to be dragged down by the burden of a litter. Now, not after breeding, is the best time to increase her ration until she achieves ideal weight.

Optimum muscle tone is also important. A bitch whose muscles are in tight, hard condition is likely to have fewer complications. It's usually not difficult to get Toy Fox Terriers to exercise. Thankfully, ours is a lively, energetic breed. Still, make sure your bitch gets sufficient exercise. You want her in the peak of condition. Exercise can be especially useful in helping to trim

74

This beauty is Gr. Ch. "PR" Meadowood's Ms. Melody, owned by John Davidson, of Dunlap, Illinois.

the figure of an overweight bitch. If your Toy Fox Terrier bitch would rather relax on the sofa, you'll have to encourage her to exercise. Toss a ball or a frisbee, or take her for a daily walk. While she may be reluctant to exercise on her own, chances are she'll be delighted at the prospect of spending some time with you. She'll feel better and you'll feel more confident in breeding her.

COORDINATING WITH THE STUD DOG OWNER

Contact the owner of the stud you have selected as soon as your bitch begins her season. There's nothing as frustrating, to a stud owner, as receiving a frantic telephone call announcing that a bitch must be bred immediately. Stud dog owners have busy lives, too. Courtesy and thoughtfulness will go a long way toward friendly relations. If you aren't certain of the exact day your bitch's season began, let the stud dog's owner know. He can arrange for you to deliver the bitch a few days early.

UNDERSTANDING YOUR BITCH'S SEASON

It's an aid to breeders to have a basic understanding of their female's heat, or estrus, cycle. If we have a general grasp of how the bitch's body functions during the breeding season, it will make it easier to determine the optimum days for breeding.

Your bitch will be in season for approximately eighteen to twenty-one days. Young bitches may, the first time, have an immature, or incomplete, season of shorter duration. It's easy to miss the first few days of a bitch's season, so close attention is essential. Your first indication that your bitch is in season will likely be the sight of a few drops of blood. You'll also note that her vulva swells, although at this early stage it will feel firm when touched. Some bitches are quite adept at keeping themselves clean. If you suspect that your bitch is in season, you may want to line her kennel or crate with a white cloth (an old sheet or white towel is ideal) so that you will be able to confirm your

Gr. Ch. "PR" Bay Toys Noel of Windy Acres is one of the fine brood bitches from Loren and Shirley Stroud's Windy Acres Kennel, in Victoria, Texas.

A very pregnant "PR" Cody's Crystal, owned by W.D. and Dorothy Cody, of Tulsa, Oklahoma. The day after this photo was taken, Crystal gave birth to five pups.

suspicions. Some bitches have a pinkish discharge, but most show bright red blood.

During this first phase, you may notice behavioral changes in your TFT female. Some bitches become anxious and nervous, while others seem overly affectionate. A bitch may be a bit testy with other females. Don't be surprised if she needs to go out to relieve herself more often than usual. These changes are due to the sudden production of hormones and are quite normal. This first phase of your bitch's season will last approximately one week. You should be aware, however, that all Toy Fox Terrier bitches are individuals and many vary from this general guideline.

The second phase of the season is the one that most concerns breeders. It is during this time that the bitch is ready to be bred. By this time, your bitch's vaginal secretion will have changed. Most likely it will become clear or take on a yellowish tinge (breeders often refer to this as "straw-colored"). A light touch of your bitch's vulva, with a piece of toilet paper, will help you to observe this change. If your bitch happens to be one of those who are fastidiously clean, the best time to check is while she's sleeping or the minute she awakens. You'll notice changes in the vulva, too. It will generally show greater swelling and will be softer and almost flabby in nature. The vaginal opening will be more prominent.

The bitch's demeanor will definitely change during the second phase. She'll flirt eagerly with other dogs. If you have her in an enclosure with other bitches, you may find that they are mounting her. Some females become quite brazen in their flirtations. Owners must exercise caution during this phase of the bitch's cycle. Not only is the bitch intensely interested in being bred, but she's extremely enticing to males. The odor of her urine will proclaim to every male that she's available. Indeed, you may find a pack of males camped out on your front lawn.

Watch closely for your bitch to exhibit the classic, telltale sign of breeding readiness...flagging her tail. She will raise her tail and flip it slightly to the side. She'll also elevate her vulva in anticipation. It's best to breed a couple of days after the bitch begins flagging her tail. This is usually on the tenth to the thirteenth day. Treat this on an individual basis. Let the bitch's behavior be your guide. Most breeders breed one day, skip a day, and then repeat the breeding. This increases their chances of selecting a day when the bitch will have ovulated.

Don't assume that your bitch's interest in males will diminish after she's been bred. Continue to exercise caution in protecting her. Your bred bitch could still slip out under a fence. Males have been known to go to extraordinary lengths in their efforts to reach a female in season. You must remain vigilant.

During the final phase of your bitch's season, she will no longer be willing to stand for breeding. She may growl or snap at any male who attempts to mount her. Her swelling will diminish and her decreasing discharge will have changed to a dull brown color. Her body is now returning to normal.

As we've said, all TFT bitches are individuals. Some simply don't follow the commonly accepted rules. There are bitches who routinely have irregular seasons. They may be ready for breeding on the second day of their season. Conversely, one occasionally finds a bitch who should be bred on the sixteenth day. It's very difficult to ascertain the optimum breeding day for such females. You may breed this type of bitch, season after season, without getting her to conceive. You may want to coordinate with your veterinarian. He can perform vaginal smears that will help to pinpoint the ideal day for breeding.

DETERMINING PREGNANCY

The breeding has taken place and now the waiting game begins. If this will be your first litter, you'll undoubtedly be anxious. You'll be watching eagerly for any sign that your bitch is pregnant. I'm afraid there is nothing to do but relax. During the first month of pregnancy, there's virtually no way to tell for certain if your female has conceived.

The standard gestation period for dogs is 63 days. This is calculated from the date of the first breeding. I've found, however, that the majority of Toy Fox Terriers usually whelp before this date. Most of my females whelp about two full calendar months after their first breeding, or 60 to 61 days. I have had a few rare bitches deliver their puppies at 56 days. On rare occasions, I've also had bitches who carried their puppies longer than 63 days. I make it a practice to watch my females very closely when they reach their eighth week.

You may be able to detect signs of pregnancy as early as the fourth week. At this stage, you might note a thickening in the width of the loin.

During the fifth week, other changes may become evident. Your bitch may become ravenous, eating her food with great relish. Bitches, particularly those carrying large litters, may look fuller in the belly. It's during the fifth week of pregnancy that you can palpate the bitch in an attempt to feel the developing fetuses. Some breeders are very skilled at

Gr. Ch. "PR" Gorden's Madam Butterfly, owned by Doug and Betty Gorden, of Crosby, Texas.

78

palpation, while others just don't have the touch. The same applies to veterinarians. Palpation is effective only in the fifth week for at this stage the fetuses are small, hard and firm. Later, they will be too soft to detect. You should also know that if the bitch is carrying her puppies high up under the ribs, you won't be able to detect them. If you are going to palpate, above all, be gentle. You want to know if there are puppies. The last thing you want to do is harm them. With your thumb and index finger, gently feel along the bitch's abdomen. You are searching for one or more bumps approximately the size of a hickory nut. Once again, palpation is not foolproof. Don't become discouraged if you can't feel anything.

Ch. "PR" Hopkins' Fashionette, one of the fine females from Eliza Hopkins' kennel.

During the sixth week, you should be able to see definite signs of pregnancy. Your bitch may well have a big belly by the sixth week. Because of the added weight, her topline may begin to sag. Even bitches with strong, sound rears may appear spraddle-legged and cowhocked. You may see that the bitch's nipples are slightly swollen and appear more prominent. The breasts may begin to fill with milk. Remember, however, that your bitch could be carrying a single puppy. Do watch her closely even if you fear that she may not have conceived.

CARING FOR THE MOTHER-TO-BE

Your bitch is now eating for herself and her puppies, and you'll have to feed her accordingly. Most breeders have, over the years, developed different diets for use on pregnant bitches. Ask ten different breeders what they feed and you're bound to get ten different answers. This only illustrates that there is no one specific way of feeding that will insure success. There are, however, certain general guidelines that you should follow.

You will, of course, be increasing the amount of food your bitch will receive. Most importantly, you want to increase the quality of her food. Foods high in protein, with a good calcium content, are recommended. The important thing to remember is to make certain that you are using a complete, well-balanced dog ration. Some breeders give a vitamin and mineral supplement. Be aware that loading her up with additional vitamins is risky, however. Oversupplementation can cause many problems.

Two weeks after my females have been bred, I switch them to a high protein dog food. I've had good results by mixing this, in equal parts, with a puppy chow to supply more calcium. I prefer to moisten the food with warm water. I also begin to add canned meat or a mix of meat and a semi-moist food. This is fed once daily.

From the fourth week of pregnancy on, I give my brood bitches two feedings per day. I follow up by giving them one-half cup of milk after every feeding. I use a powdered milk that's formulated for feeding baby calves and is fortified with vitamins and minerals. My dogs also have access to plenty of fresh, clean water.

During the early stages of her pregnancy, your bitch can continue with her routine exercise. If she has good muscle tone, the whelping will be easier. By the fourth week, however, it's best to cut down on any really strenuous exercise. Jumping should definitely be curtailed. If your TFT is a house dog, it's best to stop her from jumping on and off furniture at this time. As her bulk increases, she'll be less agile and she could injure herself. As she becomes increasingly heavy, you'll have to take added precautions. You may want to separate her from the other dogs and allow her to exercise alone.

I generally curtail exercise during the final week to ten days of pregnancy. My females are brought from the kennel into the house. This allows me to keep a closer eye on them. It also allows them to become accustomed to the whelping box and begin to feel relaxed. I place my pregnant bitches in exercise runs by themselves. If a bitch is extremely large, I will all but eliminate exercise, during the final week or so.

Unless absolutely necessary, the bitch should receive no medications or shots during her pregnancy. Some medications can cause birth defects. There have been instances where treatment has been toxic and fatal to the developing fetuses. Unless the condition threatens to endanger the bitch's life, try to delay any medications until after she's whelped her litter.

Toy Fox Terriers are, generally, healthy and hardy dogs. They usually experience few problems during their pregnancies. Your best bet for avoiding problems during pregnancy is to begin with a healthy bitch. By conditioning her carefully, insuring correct exercise and feeding her sensibly, you will have prepared her for her job as a mother. As the date she's due to whelp approaches, watch her closely. By being vigilant, you'll be able to see both the physical and behavioral changes, and avoid any problems.

10

Having Puppies

Delivering a litter of puppies is a natural process for your bitch. We've all heard the stories of bitches that whelped their litters, without assistance, under the porch of an old farm house. There's even the old timer's story of the Foxhound bitch. It seems that the pregnant bitch was part of a pack in hot pursuit of their quarry. During the chase, the bitch stopped, whelped a puppy and cleaned it off. Taking it in her mouth, she rejoined the other pack members, continued the chase and then came home to deliver the rest of her litter.

Natural though it may be, some dogs do need assistance in bringing their puppies into the world. Toy dogs may encounter more problems than larger breeds. It's advisable for you to be there, just in case there's a problem. Toy Fox Terriers are, in general, excellent mothers. Some do, however, need a little help in getting started.

If this is the first time you've attended a mother-to-be, it's natural that you'll be nervous. Just don't let your anxiety consume you. Some bitch owners have panicked at the last moment and rushed the bitch to the veterinarian, so he could do the whelping. The place for the bitch who's beginning labor is at home, unless complications force a trip to the vet. She'll be more relaxed in familiar surroundings.

Your best bet for staying calm is to educate yourself. If you know what to anticipate, the whole experience will seem less frightening to you. By learning as much as possible about what will happen, you'll be able to tell when things are going awry. It's impossible to predict how your bitch will act, particularly if this is her first litter. She may take command of the situation and not need any assistance at all. If she has the situation well in hand, don't interfere.

As the big day approaches, you're likely to become more and more anxious. Take heart for most whelpings go smoothly, just as nature intended. To allay your fears, refer to this chapter and gather all the equipment that you might need. If you have a friend who's a long time breeder, keep the telephone close by. Many an experienced breeder has talked a novice through the process. If you truly fear that there might be a problem, check with your veterinarian. Tell him the date your bitch is due and make sure that he will be there or on call, should you need him during the night.

WHERE TO HAVE THE PUPPIES

Left to her own devices, the bitch will surely choose an inappropriate place to whelp. Stories of bitches who delivered their litters in closets, in a dryer with the door left ajar, under the living room sofa, or in the middle of a bed, abound. Give some thought to where you want to house the mom and her litter. You want a place that's free from drafts and reasonably warm. Most importantly, you want a place where mom can feel secure and where she'll stay calm. Look for a spot that's away from the hustle and bustle of everyday life. You'll also want a location where you can easily glance in and check on her. If you have a guest bedroom, or there's a convenient corner of your bedroom, this may be ideal. It's possible that you'll have several nights when you'll be half-awake, watching the bitch. Having access to a bed, for naps, is handy. If at all possible, you'll want a telephone within easy reach, just in case you do have an emergency.

Your bitch needs to feel protected and secure. This isn't the time to plan a dinner party or issue an invitation to the family to come for a visit. Keep strangers and friends alike away from the bitch. Don't bring people in to see the expectant mother. If there are children in your home, declare the mother-to-be's room strictly off limits. Expectant mothers have been known to act unpredictably.

It's best to provide the bitch with a whelping box. There are many types of boxes, some fancy and some simple, that may be used for the bitch. My whelping boxes are made of plywood and wire and measure 24 inches long, 15 inches wide and 18 inches high. I use a light bulb, which remains on during the whelping and for the next several days, to provide extra warmth.

Some breeders elect to use cardboard cartons for their whelping bitches. These are readily available from a grocery store. If you decide to go this route, be absolutely sure you know what came in the cartons. You must never use cartons which formerly contained a potentially toxic substance, such as detergents or abrasives. Cardboard cartons don't hold up as well as permanent whelping pens, so you'll need two boxes. One will be used during the actual whelping. You will transfer mom and her puppies to the other box after they've been born. You'll have to cut an opening in one side of the box, leaving a strip along the bottom about two to three inches high. This will allow mom to get away from the puppies and yet keep them from tumbling out.

Chances are, those with several bitches will opt for permanent whelping boxes. Each breeder seems to come up with a design that suits him. There are, however, several guidelines you should follow. You must be capable of easily sanitizing the whelping box. If you opt for cardboard cartons, these, of course, should be discarded after each use. You'll want to make sure that the mother has an opportunity to get away from the puppies. She must have easy access to them, but be able to escape their constant demands. You must decide on the bedding to line the whelping box. Some breeders opt for baby receiving

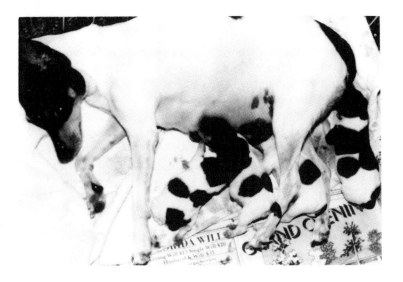

Kathleen Cornwell's Ch. "PR" Windy Acres' Tara nurses her litter of four.

blankets or indoor-outdoor carpeting. I prefer newspaper. It's easily obtainable, can be discarded when it become dirty and is inexpensive.

It's best to place the mother in the whelping box about a week before she's due to whelp. This way she can become accustomed to her new surroundings. Mothers, suddenly placed in a new and strange whelping box, have been known to try relocating their litters to a place of their own choosing. It will hasten her adjustment if you feed her in the box. Encourage her and tell her how good she is for remaining in this strange, new place. By the time she's ready to deliver the litter, she will have settled down and will be comfortable in her new home. If your bitch is dirty, bathe and dry her carefully before placing her in the whelping box.

Most TFTs will be fine in your normal household temperature. Freedom from drafts, however, is essential. You don't want to take a chance on the puppies or the mother being chilled. If you fear that drafts may be a problem, it's a good idea to partially enclose the whelping box, with cardboard or blankets, to keep out the breeze. You'll want to provide extra warmth during the whelping and for the first few days. This can be provided with a light bulb, such as I use, or a heating pad on the "low" setting. One caution if you opt for a heating pad. Make certain that the mother cannot get at the electric cord. It's also a good idea to make certain that the heating pad does not cover the entire surface of the whelping pen. Tiny puppies can become overheated and they must have room to move off the heating pad or they will become dehydrated. If your bitch is whelping in winter and there's a heavy wind outside, you may want to place a small heater in the room where she's whelping. This will protect mom and babies until the weather warms again.

WHAT ELSE WILL I NEED?

It's best to collect a few supplies that may come in handy during the whelping. Have a good supply of *newspapers* on hand and a large *garbage bag* for bundling up the soiled papers. It's a good idea to have a *small cardboard box* with a heat source. Some mothers become restless while they're whelping. You may want to remove one or more puppies and place them in this box, while she delivers the next addition. You'll want to have a couple of *towels,* for cleaning and rubbing down the puppies. A pair of blunt nose *scissors* is excellent for use in cutting the umbilical cords. You might also prefer to have a *hemostat* on hand, for clamping the cord before you make the cut. Some breeders prefer to use *dental floss* to tie off the cords. It's best, just in case, to have some *Esbilac* or other milk replacer. You'll also want a *baby scale*, for weighing the newborns and a *pen* and some *paper* for jotting down notes.

HOW MANY PUPPIES CAN I EXPECT?

As far as I know, no one has ever taken a survey to determine the exact number of puppies contained in the average Toy Fox Terrier litter. From my experience (based on breeding bitches which conform, in size, to the standard), I would say that two to three puppy litters are the most common. We've had a few litters containing six puppies, but these are rare occurrences. My bitches

Ch. "PR" Hopkins' Gay Tammy poses with her history making litter. This litter, which included Ch. "PR" Hopkins' Gay Danny and Ch. "PR" Hopkins' Gay Dottie, was the first born with a three generation, all champion pedigree. This record making litter was bred by Eliza Hopkins.

have produced several litters of five puppies and many of four pups. Don't be discouraged even though your bitch doesn't appear to be pregnant. Litters of one are fairly common with Toy Fox Terriers.

There's really no way that you can guess, in advance, how many puppies your bitch will produce. It is possible to have your bitch x-rayed, but sometimes the results are inaccurate. It's better to just wait and see.

YOU AND YOUR VETERINARIAN

We hope that you've already established a close working relationship with your veterinarian. It's reassuring to know that you have someone you can trust, if need be. Don't pester your vet with calls over trivial, insignificant matters as the day of birth approaches. You don't want to gain a reputation as "the boy who cried wolf." Make sure you keep records, such as the days your bitch was bred and the hour she went into labor. These will be helpful to your veterinarian, should treatment be necessary.

Let common sense be your guide in contacting your veterinarian for help. Some vets will tell you not to worry if the bitch hasn't gone into hard labor (had at least one contraction). However, if you honestly believe there's a problem, do make a call. You are within your rights in insisting that the veterinarian meet you at his office. Trust your instincts. While your veterinarian is a well-trained professional, you live with the bitch daily and know her better than anyone else. If you're sure there's a problem, don't hesitate to pick up the phone.

WATCHING FOR THE SIGNS

Toy Fox Terrier bitches vary in the warning they will give you as the time of birth approaches. Some exhibit virtually no symptoms. Conversely, other bitches will drive you to distraction several days before the big event. Many bitches become excited, nervous and restless as the big day approaches. There are a few, however, who will remain calm until they go into labor.

One of the early signs to look for is your bitch's attempt to "nest." She'll tear papers frantically, then lie down. In a few minutes she'll be up again, ripping at the papers with her paws and mouth. She continually rearranges the papers to suit herself. Many bitches refuse food, as the time approaches. Some wolf down their food voraciously, only to regurgitate it, afterward. You may notice that your bitch is shivering violently, even though the temperature in the room is very warm. Sometimes you can detect a physical change in your bitch's appearance. She may be carrying her puppies lower and have a "hollow" look in the loin area.

Some bitches, particularly household pets, want you near them at this time. Give your TFT a few pats of encouragement, try to calm her down and tell her how well she's doing. Stay calm yourself. This period, known as prelabor, may last only an hour or the bitch may carry on like this for a day or more.

TFTs are generally excellent mothers. Here, "PR" Cornwell's Heather, owned by
Chet and Kathleen Cornwell, of Aripeka, Florida, poses with her son, Adam.

TEMPERATURE CAN BE AN INDICATOR

Most breeders will rely on their experience in determining when a bitch
is due to whelp. For the beginner, however, charting your bitch's temperature
can be helpful. The bitch's temperature will drop shortly before the birth of the
puppies. By taking her temperature repeatedly, you'll have advance warning.

The dog's normal temperature is around 101.6 degrees. Individual dogs,
however, can vary slightly from the accepted norm. For this reason, it's best to
take your bitch's temperature twice a day during the week before she's due to
whelp. Take your readings at 12 hour intervals, such as 7:00 a.m. and 7 p.m.
Avoid taking the reading immediately after your bitch has exercised, as activity
may elevate the temperature. Don't be alarmed if her temperature fluctuates
slightly during the day. This is normal. By taking her temperature in this
manner, you'll be establishing a "baseline" that will tell you what is normal for
your dog.

When you notice a steep drop in the bitch's temperature, you'll want to
watch her closely. The temperature will probably drop into the nineties. This
is a clear sign that your bitch will whelp some time within the next 24 hours.
If you see no symptoms of labor within a day after the temperature drops, phone
your veterinarian. Similarly, if your bitch has not whelped by the 63rd day after
breeding, it's best to take her in for a check-up.

LABOR BEGINS

During the first stage of labor, your bitch will become increasingly
nervous and uncomfortable. She'll scratch frantically at her papers, lie down

and pant for a few seconds and then get up to paw the papers again. She may have a pained look on her face. Don't be alarmed if she whines and trembles. Watch for your bitch to begin licking her vulva. You don't want to interfere with her at this stage. It's best to keep an eye on her from a discreet distance. Don't add to her nervousness.

The beginning stage of labor may last one hour or more. You might try speeding up the process, by letting the bitch outside to relieve herself. Offer her a drink of water. Do, however, exercise caution and keep a close eye on her while she's outside. More than one breeder has discovered that the bitch whelped a puppy outside.

If your bitch remains in this first stage of labor for more than 24 hours, call your veterinarian. Problems don't usually occur until the bitch has gone into hard labor, but it's best to be on the safe side. Do keep an eye out for an abnormal discharge. If you see a greenish or black discharge, phone the vet immediately. Excessive bleeding should also be reported promptly to your veterinarian.

HARD LABOR

Hard labor begins when your bitch has her first contraction. The first contractions could be mild and easily missed, so watch tlosely. You don't want to interfere, but it's best, at this stage, to move closer and keep a steady eye on her. Jot down the time you noticed the first contraction. Don't trust your memory. The contractions will probably increase as your bitch bears down. The contractions may follow one right after the other or there may be an interval of time between them. Much of this depends on where the puppies are, in relation to the birth canal. If this is the first time you've witnessed a bitch in labor, it may look as though she's straining to have a bowel movement. Your bitch will choose a position that's comfortable for her. Some bitches have their puppies lying down and some prefer to stand.

If your bitch is having very hard contractions and she hasn't whelped a puppy in an hour, it's time to call the veterinarian. There may be an overly large puppy that she's unable to expel. It's also possible that a puppy is in an awkward position and jammed at the entrance to the birth canal. In either of these situations, you vet may elect to perform a Caesarian section. If your bitch's hard contractions stop suddenly and don't resume within an hour, call the veterinarian.

THEY'RE HERE!

After one or several hard contractions, a large, black, bubble-like sac will emerge from the vulva. This will probably be the water bag. The appearance of the water bag is an important sign, for it signals the entrance of the first puppy into the birth canal. Be alert, for the puppy usually follows quickly. Occasionally, the water bag will burst in the birth canal, but this is not a cause for alarm.

Most puppies are born head first. The puppy will be encased in a watertight, fluid filled sac. During the months of pregnancy, he has been suspended in this fluid and received oxygen through his umbilical cord. The sac must be torn away from the puppy's head immediately, so that he can breathe air, not fluid, now that the umbilical cord is no longer providing him with oxygen. Make sure the bitch attends to this immediately. If she doesn't, tear the sac away with your fingers. Move quickly. Try to be unobtrusive, so as to avoid upsetting the bitch unnecessarily.

Generally, the bitch will take over. She'll pull away and eat the sac. She'll lick the puppy all over, cleaning it and stimulating it. You will be surprised at how roughly the bitch handles the newborn. She may even roll the puppy over, causing it to cry out and thrash around. Don't be alarmed. This is natural and beneficial. As the pup cries out, he's filling his newborn lungs with oxygen.

When the bitch has finished cleaning the puppy, she should attend to the umbilical cord. She will sever it with her teeth. If your bitch is old and has missing teeth, you'll have to step in and take over this duty. Similarly, some inexperienced mothers neglect to cut the cord. Take a firm hold on the cord, but do not pull it as this will result in an umbilical hernia. Approximately one to two inches from the puppy's belly is where you want to cut the cord. Some breeders prefer to clamp the cord first with a hemostat. If you opt for this method, leave the clamp in place for a few minutes or until the bleeding subsides. Some breeders also feel it's best to tie the cord. If you want to tie the cord, encircle it with dental floss and make one or two knots. Be sure to cut off all the excess floss. If you don't trim the floss, it will worry the mother and she may tug on it and injure the puppy.

Be sure to look for the placenta, or afterbirth. This is usually attached to the umbilical cord. The afterbirth is about half the size of the puppy and will resemble a dark piece of liver. Occasionally, the placenta will separate from the puppy and be expelled just after he's born or be pushed out by the emergence of the next puppy.

You'll want to be alert for the appearance of each afterbirth. There will be one for every puppy born. You may want to make a note each time you see one. After the whelping is completed, check your notes. If an afterbirth was not expelled, contact your veterinarian. Retained placentas cause very serious infection and may be fatal to your bitch.

Breeders differ in their opinions as to whether the mother should be allowed to eat the afterbirths. The afterbirth is a rich source of vitamins and nutrients. In the wild, it supplies the mother with nourishment, so that she doesn't have to leave the litter in search of food. Experts also believe that the placenta may stimulate milk production. Unfortunately, consuming the afterbirth has a laxative effect on the bitch and she's apt to have loose stools for a few days. Some breeders remove and discard all afterbirths. Many breeders allow the bitch to eat one afterbirth and remove all subsequent ones. Some breeders believe it's best to allow the bitch to consume as many as she wants. Talk with your veterinarian, or friends who are experienced breeders, to help you decide what to do.

CLEARING THE PUPPY OF FLUID

Once the mother has cleaned up the puppy, you'll want to pick him up and examine him. Some mothers object to this, while others seem to welcome the help. If the mother objects and you feel she's done a good job, you can delay. Rub the puppy vigorously, with a towel, until he's completely dried. Remember, you needn't be gentle. If he hasn't made a sound or if he seems a little sluggish, give a sharp little tug on his tail. This is akin to spanking a newborn human infant on the bottom. He'll cry out and his lungs will fill with oxygen.

Hold the puppy to your ear. If you hear any rasping, rattling or bubbling, the puppy has retained fluid in its lungs. You don't want him to get pneumonia, so it's best to deal with this immediately. You'll want to "swing down" or "shake down" the puppy, as breeders call this technique. While it may sound complicated, once you try it, you'll see how simple it is in reality. Hold the puppy very securely, with his belly resting in your palm. Place the other hand over its back, with the index finger and middle finger behind the puppy's neck and head for support. Stand up straight with your legs approximately shoulder's width apart. Carefully raise the puppy, at arm's length, over your head. Make sure your grip is secure, you don't want to drop him. Swing your arms forcefully in an arc, from over your head to down between your legs. The centrifugal force

"PR" Casas Adobe's Amber, owned by Judy Guillot, of Tucson, Arizona, at one day of age. (David Ring photo)

generated in this maneuver will expel fluid from the puppy's lungs. You'll notice a few bubbles of moisture at the puppy's nose and/or mouth. Wipe these off and repeat the procedure. Place the puppy to your ear once again. If you still hear rasping, repeat the procedure. Continue with this until the puppy's lungs sound clear.

THE FAMILY GROWS

Bitches may deliver their puppies in rapid succession, or there could be a lengthy break before the next puppy arrives. It will calm the bitch if you leave the puppy with her, until the next contractions begin. Many bitches become restless when the contractions start again. They stand, walk around and tear at the papers. It's best to remove the first puppy, so that mom can concentrate on the task at hand. You wouldn't want her to lie on the pup or inadvertently injure him. Be sure to place him on a heating pad or under a heat lamp.

It's entirely possible that the second puppy may come "breech" or feet first. Such births are fairly common in dogs. Breech puppies may come easily. There is the possibility, however, that the puppy may hang up since the widest part of his body (the shoulders) exits last. Some bitches must give an extra push or two to expel the pup. If the hind legs emerge, but the rest of the pup does not immediately follow, you should help. Grasp the hind legs and hold them securely. If at all possible, leave the sac intact. Pull gently, steadily and very slowly. It's best to pull in time with the mother's contractions. If she isn't bearing down, massage her stomach to stimulate the contractions. Make certain you pull out and down, just as the puppy would come into the world naturally. Once the puppy is out, quickly break the sac, clean and massage the puppy, and swing him down. This is very important, as breech puppies almost always have fluid in their lungs.

Experienced breeders can often successfully turn a puppy which is in an abnormal position inside the mother. They've learned this skill from watching veterinarians, talking with breeders and, most of all, through experience. It's difficult for novices to deal with this type of problem, however. A call to your veterinarian is in order.

HELPING THE PUPPIES TO NURSE

Now that the puppies are here, it's time for them to nurse. Some puppies instinctively hunt for a nipple, almost immediately, while others may not nurse for an hour or more. First time mothers may be uncomfortable having the puppies nurse. Don't worry, with time and patience, the bitch will catch on.

The first feeding is very important. Following birth, the mother produces colostrum. This milky substance contains antibodies that transfer the mother's immunity to the puppies. If a puppy seems reluctant to nurse, you'll have to lend a helping hand. Open the puppy's mouth and place it on a nipple. Squeeze a few drops of milk onto the puppy's tongue. If necessary, support his body while he

What could be more charming than a TFT puppy? Robbie Overstreet, of Richmond, Texas, holds 8 week old Thomas Jefferson in the palm of her hand. He weighs a single pound.

nurses. Getting a newborn to nurse is sometimes frustrating, but just keep at it. Soon you'll be rewarded by a row of contented little puppies with full tummies.

THE CAESARIAN BITCH

We hope that your bitch won't need a Caesarian section, but just in case, there are a few special tips for handling a C-section bitch and her family. Much of the success of the Caesarian will depend upon your veterinarian. There's no denying that some veterinarians are more skilled than others in performing this operation. Techniques vary. Some vets make a small incision, while others make a very large cut. It is absolutely essential that your veterinarian be well schooled in administering anesthesia to toy dogs. Sad to say, some bitches have been overdosed and failed to regain consciousness.

The veterinarian will probably have an assistant to help him, during the operation. If he can't contact someone on short notice, you may have to assist. The vet will handle the bitch and you'll see to the puppies. Dry them off and swing them, if necessary, just as you would in a natural birth.

It's difficult to predict how quickly your bitch will regain consciousness. Much depends on how much anesthesia the veterinarian has used. Discuss this with the vet. Ask him how long you can expect the bitch to be affected and call him back if she hasn't roused in that time. Keep the bitch warm until she comes completely out from the effects of the anesthesia.

Caesarian mothers sometimes have trouble accepting their puppies. Bitches who have already had a litter will adapt more readily to the situation.

91

They've had puppies before and will usually respond to their natural mothering instincts. If this is your bitch's first litter, things could be a bit tricky. Remember, she's just come through a very stressful situation. She remembers being in pain. She was then whisked away to a strange place with unusual smells, someone gave her a shot and she remembers nothing else. If this is her first litter, she's never seen newborn puppies before. They are strange little things and they've been placed in her pen (which she views as her territory). Chances are the puppies are crying or making unusual sounds that are new to her. Under these conditions, the bitch may move aggressively on the puppies. You must be there to intervene. She'll get used to them, but it will take a little time. Hold her down, if you must. Get the puppies as close to mom as you can. The sooner they start to smell like her, the sooner she'll accept them.

Caesarian puppies will have absorbed some of the anesthesia. Therefore, they will be a little more sluggish than vaginally born puppies. You may have to work longer to get them to successfully nurse. To make matters more complicated, the mother is apt to be sore and may be reluctant to have them nurse. Gradually, the bitch will accept her new charges. Be sure not to let your sympathy for the bitch, and her ordeal, get the best to you. Insist that she take care of her babies.

11

The Mother & Her Family

Now that the excitement of whelping is past, you'll be able to settle down and observe mom and her brood. Newborn puppies will nurse and sleep around the clock, during these first few days. You'll be amazed at how quickly they grow. Don't be surprised if the little whelps double in size before your eyes. If the bitch has the situation well in hand, don't interfere. This is not the time for visitors, so don't invite people over to see the babies. Do watch the puppies. You'll be able to determine when something is amiss. Healthy, vital puppies will wriggle and squirm when you pick them up. The weak, listless, limp puppy, who cries incessantly, is a problem. He may not be getting enough milk. It's also best to keep an extra close eye on any very tiny pups in the litter. Make sure that they aren't being pushed off the nipple by their stronger littermates. If necessary, place them on the nipple and make sure they get their fair share.

Make certain the dam is cleaning the puppies. Newborn pups are unable to urinate and defecate on their own for the first few days, and mom must attend to this. She should lick and stimulate them to eliminate. If you fear that the bitch is neglecting this, you'll have to fill in for her. Dip a piece of cotton in warm water and gently rub the pups' private parts.

TAILS AND DEWCLAWS

Your little Toy Fox Terriers will be born with long, tapering tails. The best age to dock the tails is at two or three days. By waiting a couple of days, you'll ensure that all the pups are strong, healthy and off to a good start. At two to three days, the puppies' bones are still soft, and their nervous and circulatory systems are not fully developed. Puppy tails can still be docked after this time, but it takes a little longer for the puppies to recover.

It takes experience to determine precisely where the dock should be made. The standard tells us that a full three-fifths should be taken off the tail. It's best, however, to judge each puppy individually. Look and feel the tail by running your fingers down the length. You'll see and feel that the tail is broader at the base where it joins the body. You'll also note that a very short way down, the tail begins to taper. Look and feel for this point. The cut should always be made where the taper begins.

Veterinarians and breeders who go strictly by the ruler are apt to experience problems, if they have a litter which includes natural bob tails. As

Puppies learning to eat on their own. This fine litter was bred by Eliza and Phil Hopkins, in the 1960's. The sire was Nat. Gr. Ch. "PR" Currens' Sammy of Parkside and the dam was "PR" Currens' Penny of Parkside.

we've already discussed, natural bob tails rarely come in the ideal length. The chances are that you will have to remove a portion of the tail. Puppies from natural bob lines may have only a three-quarter length tail. It's easy to see that if you dock three-fifths off this shorter tail, you will end up with a tail that's too short. You'll avoid this by judging by the sight and feel of the tail, and take any excess off where it begins to taper.

You may also wish to remove the dewclaws, although this is optional. For the uninitiated, dewclaws are the extra fifth toe on the inside of the legs. Dewclaws are always found on the front feet and, occasionally, they're seen on the hind feet. I choose not to remove front dewclaws, but some show breeders prefer to remove them. They feel that the front legs have a cleaner, neater appearance without the dewclaws and the removal may avoid accidental injury. I do recommend removing the hind dewclaws. The dewclaws on hind legs seem to stick out more prominently than those found on the front. This makes them more liable to injury.

Most experienced breeders have learned to dock their own puppy tails and remove dewclaws. Novice breeders will likely rely on their veterinarians. If you wish to dock your own puppy tails, it's best to contact an experienced breeder and have him demonstrate the procedure.

It is a good idea to keep the puppies away from their mother if the tails are bleeding. The bleeding is apt to upset mom and, in her anxiety, she may chew at the tail. If the tails were stitched, she could inadvertently pull the

94

stitches loose. Keep the puppies warm while they're away from their mother. The bleeding will soon abate and they can be returned.

THE NURSING MOTHER

In the days following the whelping, keep an eye on the mother. It's natural for her to have some discharge, usually reddish brown in color. She may also continue to bleed. If you notice excessive bleeding, particularly if it's bright red blood, contact your veterinarian. Be alert for any sign of a greenish discharge. This type of discharge usually means that a placenta has been retained and could spell serious trouble, if not treated promptly. If the mother seems weak or listless, has an elevated temperature, or goes into convulsions, take her immediately to the veterinarian.

Your bitch will probably have a voracious appetite. Continue feeding her as you did when she was pregnant. Allow her to consume as much food as she wishes. Also, be certain that the bitch is supplied with plenty of clean water. You'll be surprised at how much she drinks. This is normal, don't be alarmed.

THE PUPPIES GROW

The puppies' eyes will open at about two weeks of age. It's fascinating to watch them discover their new world. By two or three weeks, they'll be staggering onto their feet and trying to take their first faltering steps. In another short week, they'll be walking without difficulty. However, if you've had a litter with only one puppy, it may take him a little longer to begin walking. You'll want to clip back the puppies' toenails at this stage. The tips can be taken off with a pair of scissors or a human nail clipper. Be careful to remove only the white tip and avoid cutting into the pink vein, known as the "quick."

WEANING TIME

Normally, I begin weaning my puppies between five and six weeks of age. Much depends on the mother's attitude. Some mothers grow fussy during the fourth week and don't want the puppies to nurse. Conversely, other mothers will stay with their pups well into the seventh week, even allowing them to nurse once the sharp milk teeth have emerged. Generally, mothers with a single puppy will continue to nurse for a longer period.

Most Toy Fox Terrier puppies are avid eaters and your litter will probably take less than a week to wean. You might want to begin with a small dish of milk. It's best to give this in a shallow bowl. Stick the puppies' noses in the liquid and they will usually begin to lap.

While some breeders wait, I start my puppies on solid food at the same time I offer the milk. The puppies are given their first taste of food while their mother is placed outside for exercise. I offer them the same mixture I've been feeding the mother, with its' meat topping (see Caring for the Mother-to-Be).

Don't be surprised if your puppies are messy. They'll take a few bites of the food, walk in it, fall in it and, generally have a wonderful time making absolute messes of themselves. You may need to stir and loosen the food, since their trampling will pack it and make it difficult for them to eat. When they loose interest in the food, return mom to them. She'll finish up the remainder of the meal, including what's on the pups.

Approximately a week after the puppies are weaned, I gradually decrease the amount of canned milk they are receiving. I begin to offer them lukewarm water instead. They are now receiving the milk powder contained in the puppy chow and I wish to avoid the risk of causing diarrhea. Diarrhea can be a serious problem for young puppies, as it can lead to dehydration. Make sure to check with your veterinarian and have him prescribe medication to clear up the situation, if it develops.

I continue feeding my puppies three times daily, until they reach eight to nine weeks of age. Some breeders prefer to give four feedings at this stage. At eight to nine weeks, I begin to stir the mixture thoroughly together. At this stage, the puppies are capable of eating the moistened dry food, and I don't want them to fill up on the meat topping and leave the rest.

I judge when to decrease the number of feedings by how well the puppies are doing. By four months, I sometimes cut them back to two meals a day. Use your common sense in this regard and judge by the puppy. You may wish to keep those tiny puppies on three feedings a day for quite a while. I continue the twice a day feeding schedule until the puppies are one year of age.

SOCIALIZATION

As the pups grow, you'll want to give them attention. After the first week or so, you'll probably pick them up, cuddle them and love them, while mom is out exercising. Puppies need love to grow into stable adults with charming

These pups, bred by John Davidson, of Dunlap, Illinois, are beginning to explore the world.

What's the best present to find in your Christmas stocking? TFT puppies, of course. Lori and Crystal McConnell show off "PR" McConnell's Robin and "PR" McConnell's Miss Piggy. These two lovely pups were bred by Dianne McConnell, of Clovis, New Mexico.

personalities. You may want to expose them to household sounds. The television, radio and vacuum cleaner, as well as the clatter of pots and pans, and the ringing of the telephone, may startle and frighten them at first, but they'll quickly adjust.

If the weather is warm, pups can be taken out at about five weeks of age. Be sure, however, that they have access to the shade. You may want to provide them with toys. An old work glove or discarded sock makes an excellent and inexpensive play toy. While they love squeaky toys, it's best not to allow them to play with these. They could tear apart the toy and accidentally swallow the squeaker.

EARS

There's no way to predict precisely when your puppies' ears will come up. Some pups have their ears up by the time they're weaned, but others may take longer. Generally, ears will come up more quickly on the smaller pups in the litter. The size of the ears often varies from bloodline to bloodline. A puppy with larger sized ears will be slower to bring them up. I have, on rare occasions, had a puppy whose ears didn't come up until one year of age. Most puppies, however, will have their ears standing by about five months.

Stress can have a perplexing effect on ears. Even pups with strongly standing ears may drop them, when they begin to teethe. Sometimes ears will come up and go down, several times, during the teething process. It's best to avoid any additional stress until the puppy's permanent teeth are in fully and his ears are back up.

VACCINATIONS

Your puppy will gradually lose the immunity he obtained from his mother. There's no precise date when this will occur. It's best to check with your vet to see when he wishes to start the immunization program. It will probably be at six to eight weeks of age. Generally, puppy vaccinations are given as a series of two or three shots. Since there's no way to tell exactly when the mother's immunity will end, the multiple shots will ensure that the puppy is adequately protected. Don't stint or think you can save money by skipping the shots. The cost of vaccination is very small, compared to the cost of treating a dog who has contracted distemper, hepatitis or leptospirosis.

Your puppies are now well on their way to becoming well adjusted adult Toy Fox Terriers. More than likely, you'll decide to keep at least one of the litter. With a little luck, it could become your first homebred champion. The other puppies will go to loving homes. Be sure to check back, periodically, with their new owners. Go to see the puppy or request a photo. By keeping in touch with people who purchase your pups, you'll be better able to evaluate the litter. This will be of great help to you in planning your next breeding.

12

Showing Your TFT

The sport of showing dogs is a fascinating and worthwhile pastime. While it may appear that shows are merely canine beauty contests, they are actually much more. At a show, the judge compares the dogs entered to determine which most closely adheres to the ideal called for in the standard. Shows are the proving grounds where breeders gather to measure the success of their breeding programs. At a Toy Fox Terrier show, you will be able to see many TFTs competing for points toward their championships. Shows also provide an opportunity for seeing new dogs and meeting or renewing acquaintances with other people interested in Toy Fox Terriers. By attending dog shows, you will develop an eye for what constitutes a good TFT and you'll gain an appreciation for a truly fine animal.

UNDERSTANDING U.K.C. SHOWS

When you attend your first dog show, the whole judging process may seem rather bewildering and mystifying. However, United Kennel Club shows do follow a logical pattern. Dogs are entered in classes according to their sex and their age on the day of the show. Males are always judged before females and young dogs are judged before older dogs. Once you keep this simple rule in mind, you'll be able to follow the sequence of judging.

The first class to be judged is the *Puppy Class* for males that are six months to one year of age. Next comes the *Junior Class* for males. Entered in this class will be males that are one to two years of age. The *Senior Class* for males consists of dogs that are at least two years of age, but less than three years. The last males to judged are those entered in the *Veterans Class*. These are males over three years of age. After the Veteran's Class has been judged, the winners of the Puppy, Junior, Senior and Veterans classes will be brought into the ring to compete against one another. The judge will select one male as *Best Male of Show*. The same classes, in the same order and with the same age requirements, are then judged for female TFTs. After the class judging, the female winners of all the classes will be brought to the ring, and the judge will select the *Best Female of Show*. After the *Best Female of Show* has been selected, she will be joined in the ring by the *Best Male of Show*. These two dogs will compete against each other and the winner will be proclaimed *Best of Show*.

Most Toy Fox Terrier shows include a *Champion of Champions Class.* This special class is judged following the selection of Best of Show. Males and females compete against each other in this class, which consists of dogs who have already earned their U.K.C. championship titles. Unlike the regular classes, U.K.C. rules require that the Champion of Champions class be entered, by mail, in advance. The date for the closing of entries will be listed in the Club's advertisement for the show. Advance entry is required to insure that there will be sufficient competition. At least five Toy Fox Terrier champions must be pre-entered and a minimum of three must be present in the ring on the day of the show. The winner of this class is declared *Best Champion of Show.*

Next, comes the *Grand Champions Class.* In order to qualify for this class, a Toy Fox Terrier must have already earned the U.K.C. Grand Champion title. Although advance entries are not always required, the club holding the show may insist that dogs be entered, by mail, in advance. At least two Grand Champions must compete in order for this class to be held.

Twice annually, the National Toy Fox Terrier Association has shows. At these national shows, the Grand Champions class takes on a special meaning. For these two shows, the class is always advance entered and there must be at least five pre-entries, with three dogs actually competing. The victor is declared a *National Grand Champion* and receives a special degree from the U.K.C. This is a highly coveted title.

Toy Fox Terrier shows may also include some non-licensed classes. These are usually held after the regular judging. They never delay the starting time for regular classes. *Puppy Classes* or *Puppy Fun Classes* for dogs under six months old, are usually offered. Many clubs also have a *Junior Handling* or *Junior Showmanship Class,* in which youngsters compete with their dogs. The club may elect to hold a *Parade of Champions,* for older champions who no longer compete in the regular classes. *Get of Sire* classes, in which studs compete along with three or four of their offspring, from different litters, may also be offered. An identical class for females, called *Produce of Dam,* may also be included.

HOW CHAMPIONSHIP TITLES ARE EARNED

The U.K.C. awards *Champion* (abbreviated as CH.) and *Grand Champion* (or GR. CH.) titles. Points toward a Championship are earned by winning first place in the Puppy, Junior, Senior or Veterans Classes. The winners of each of these classes receives ten points toward their championships. The Best Male of Show and the Best Female of Show each receive an additional fifteen points toward their titles. In addition, the dog judged Best of Show receives ten extra points. Thus, a male that won first place in the Junior Class, for example, and went on to be judged Best Male of Show and then Best of Show would win a total of 35 points toward his championship. This is the maximum number of points that can be awarded at any one show. In order to earn a championship, a Toy Fox Terrier must accumulate a total of 100 points. Furthermore, these points must have been earned under at least three different judges. For a TFT

Ch. U-CD "PR" Fishinger's Elvis poses with some of his trophies. Elvis is the first TFT to earn titles in both the conformation and obedience rings. He is shown in both rings by his owner/trainer Nancy L. Fishinger, of Orlando, Florida.

to complete the championship requirements, the dog must also have been awarded at least one Best Male or Best Female of Show enroute to the title.

The Grand Championship title is awarded to dogs who have already completed and been confirmed as U.K.C. Champions. In order to earn a Grand Championship, the dog must compete in the Champion of Champions class. He must win the Champion of Champions class in at least three shows, under three different licensed judges.

LOCATING A SHOW

How do you locate a U.K.C. sponsored show for Toy Fox Terriers? TFT shows are sponsored by individual state clubs. Those interested in showing their dogs should subscribe to the U.K.C. publication *Bloodlines*. All Toy Fox Terrier shows are advertised in this magazine. The advertisement for the show will include much information. The name of the club and the date of the show will be listed. Pay attention to the amount of the entry fee and, especially the time deadline for the closing of entries. Entries will not be accepted after this hour. The advertisement will include the name of the judge and may specify an alternate judge. There will also be additional helpful information, such as directions to the show grounds and the names of motels or hotels close to the show site. The announcement of the show will tell you whether food will be available or whether you should plan on bringing lunch from home. The names and phone numbers of one or two persons will be listed in case you need more information.

101

PROPER SHOW RING ATTIRE

You want to wear comfortable clothing that's appropriate for the season. Your clothing need not be dressy, but it should be in good taste. Avoid tight fitting clothes that may restrict your movement. Shoes are very important. They should be comfortable and practical. High heels are never appropriate for dog shows. While you may certainly wear jewelry, keep it simple. Heavy charm bracelets that clank will distract your dog and the judge. Likewise, heavy necklaces that brush against your dog, when you pose him on the table, are best left at home. Perfume or cologne should be used in moderation. While your dog may be used to the scent, it could distract another dog.

It's also best to prepare for emergencies. Be sure to take a raincoat. Even though most Toy Fox Terrier shows are held indoors, you still have to get from your car to the building. If the weather is cool, take along a warm jacket. While the building may be heated, you'll be prepared just in case the heat goes out. In rain or cold, you can also pick up your TFT and tuck him under your jacket, to keep him dry and warm until he's ready to go in the ring.

PREPARING FOR THE SHOW

You'll want to groom your dog several days before the show. Nothing is more unpleasant for a judge than to be forced to examine a dirty, smelly dog. Take pride in your dog. While you may not have the Best of Show winner on the end of your lead, you can always have the cleanest dog in the show. By following the weekly grooming schedule already outlined in the book, you will have very little to do, before the show, other than give the dog a bath. Check your dog's ears and make sure that they are clean. Check his teeth and, if necessary, clean them. Make sure you have trimmed the dog's nails and, if you've neglected this, attend to it immediately. For a week or so before the show, you may want to brush your TFT daily. A good daily brushing will give your dog's coat that desirable shine and lustre.

According to the U.K.C.'s rules, TFTs are not to be chalked. No method should be employed which will attempt to correct faulty color. Any altering of coat color, eye color, or the pigmentation of the nose or lips is strictly prohibited. The U.K.C.

In Junior Showmanship, youngsters have the opportunity to compete. Vance Saucedo is shown winning with Ch. "PR" Singleton's Mikimoto Ace, owned by Jeri Singleton, of Annapolis, Maryland. (Harkins photo)

102

recommends that the dog's whiskers be left untrimmed. While you will not be penalized for trimming the whiskers, most TFT breeders believe it serves no purpose.

You'll want to assemble all the equipment and supplies you intend to take with you. Until you become a seasoned show hand, you may want to make a list, so you won't forget anything. Be sure to take along the directions to the show and the papers for entering your dog. Pack any clothing you will need and don't forget your raincoat. You'll also want to take along some things for your dog. Be sure to take a dish for water. This can also serve as a food dish, if your dog will be eating at the show site. It's a good idea to take along a thermos of water from home, to avoid upsetting your dog's system with strange water. Most Toy Fox Terrier exhibitors bring along a crate, or kennel, for confining their

Ch. "PR" Byrd's Vicki of Parks, in a natural stack. On this day, she was judged Best Female TFT and Best of Show. Her proud owners are Ronald and Colleen Byrd, of Berger, Missouri.

dog. If you are taking several TFTs, you may also wish to bring an exercise pen for them.

A few extra items will insure your comfort at the show. You may want to bring along some folding chairs, just in case seats are in short supply, at the show grounds. If there's no concession stand, pack your own lunch. You may want to bring a cooler chest stocked with ice and sodas. Alcoholic beverages are not permitted at the show.

ENTERING YOUR DOG

You will have to enter your dog when you arrive at the show site. You will receive an entry slip from the person taking entries. Your Toy Fox Terrier must be weighed before his entry is accepted. According to the standard, TFTs must weigh between 3 1/2 and 7 pounds. However, dogs entered in the Puppy and Junior Classes will be entered although they do not reach the 3 1/2 pound minimum. If your dog's weight is acceptable, you will be permitted to enter him in the show.

You will need official documentation, from the United Kennel Club, to enter your dog. This will show that the dog is U.K.C. registered, list his owner and verify his birthdate, which will determine which class the dog should enter. Recently, the U.K.C. has begun issuing *Easy Entry Cards,* which greatly simplify the process of entering dogs in U.K.C. events. These cards are sent to the owner when a dog is permanently registered or transferred. Photostatic copies are not acceptable, so be sure to have the original papers or cards. Here is a list of the papers you will need for entering your Toy Fox Terrier in a U.K.C. show:

> For Puppy Classes (6-12 months): A green puppy certificate or a permanent registration certificate, and a pedigree.
> For other regular classes (Junior, Senior or Veterans): A registration certificate and a pedigree, or an easy entry card, signed by the owner.
> For the Champion of Champions class (always advance entered): A registration certificate or easy entry card, along with the championship degree. If the easy entry card or the registration certificate indicates that the dog is a champion, then you need not bring along proof of the degree.
> For the Grand Champion class (advance entry may be required): A registration certificate or an easy entry card, along with the Grand Champion degree. If the registration certificate or the easy entry card already indicates that the dog is a Grand Champion, then proof of the degree is not required.

Once your dog has been weighed and the information from his papers recorded, you will pay your entry fee. You will be given an armband with your entry number on it. Your dog is now officially entered in the show. If you have any questions, don't hesitate to ask the person taking the entries. They'll be more than happy to help you.

BEFORE YOU GO IN THE RING

Let your dog relax before you go into the show ring. It's a good idea to walk him, so that he can eliminate, if need be. Permit him a small drink of water. Don't let him drink too much, though, or he's apt to have a "pot bellied" look.

If you aren't in the first class, be sure to observe the judging. It can be very valuable to see how the judge organizes his ring. You'll see if he prefers to gait the dogs around the ring

Jeri Singleton, of Annapolis, Maryland, poses her Gr. Ch. "PR" Singleton's Stormy Ace on the table. (Harkins photo)

104

Gr. Ch. "PR" Byrd's Mi-Treasure, owned by Ronald and Colleen Byrd, poses for the judge. Note the placement markers in the background.

immediately or if he examines the dogs before moving them. Perhaps the judge examines all the dogs before gaiting any of them individually. Or he may examine each dog, gait him and then proceed to the next dog. By paying close attention, you'll know what to expect when it's your turn to go in the ring.

IN THE RING

When your class is called, enter the ring promptly. To allow the dogs to settle down and to provide a general impression of the class, the judge will usually have the handlers and their dogs circle the ring once or twice. The dogs will be gaited in a counterclockwise circle. Move your dog out smartly, but remember, this is not supposed to be a race. If your dog starts to run, give a little jerk on the lead to get him under control. You want the judge to see your dog moving at the pace that's best for him. Don't run into or crowd the dog in front of you. Nor should you move so slowly that you cause the dogs behind you to jam up. After one or two circuits of the ring, the judge will indicate that he wants the dogs to stop. Pay attention. By listening to the judge and observing the other handlers, you will know what is expected.

The judge will now begin his individual examinations of the dogs. Toy Fox Terriers are examined on a table. If you are first in line, pick your dog up and take him to the table promptly. If you are waiting in line, let your dog relax, but be sure to pay attention to the judge, so you'll know when it's your turn.

Once your dog is on the table, the judge will approach from the dog's front. The table examination gives the judge the opportunity to get a close-up look at your dog. He'll pay close attention to your Toy Fox Terrier's head, ears and expression. The judge will ask you to show him your dog's bite. He does not want you to open the mouth. Simply pull up the upper lip with one hand and pull down the lower lip with the other. The judge will feel your dog's shoulders and may feel for spring of rib. Some judge's will run their hand along the dog's topline and feel the coat. For males, the judge will insure that both testicles are present.

105

Most judges will examine all the dogs, on the table, before gaiting them. The judges will ask you to move your dog in one of several formations. If you've been paying attention, you will know what to expect. If yours is the first dog to be judged and you're not sure of the judge's instructions, ask him for clarification. Check your show lead to make sure it's in the proper position. Most Toy Fox Terriers are shown on a fairly loose lead. It is to your advantage to move your dog at the speed that's best for him. If your dog breaks into a gallop or acts up, you should stop. Give your dog a little jerk, to get his attention, and then begin again. Remember to keep your dog between you and the judge. Most judges will take a look at your dog, posed naturally, when he's through gaiting. Using your show lead, maneuver your TFT into an attractive stance. If he has stopped awkwardly, take a couple of steps and walk him into a better position. When the judge is through looking at your dog, he will indicate that you are to return to the line of dogs.

Some judges will have the dogs move around the ring again, before making their final selection. When he's made his decision, the judge will point to the winners. Go to the appropriate place marker and you'll receive your ribbon. If you have won your class, be sure not to leave the show. You're not through, yet. You'll be called back into the ring, after the other classes have been judged, to compete for Best Male or Best Female of Show.

BE A GOOD SPORT

You should always act in a courteous, considerate fashion at a dog show. It's very bad form to interfere with other dogs while you are in the ring. Do not allow your dog to lunge or growl at other dogs. Your dog may be excused from the ring if he becomes a nuisance. Pay attention while you're in the ring. Don't indulge in conversations with those standing at ringside. There will be plenty of time for that later. While you may talk to other handlers in the ring, keep your voice low and don't break the judge's concentration. Remember, the judge is in the ring to do a job. Don't engage him in a conversation. Some judges will barely speak with exhibitors during the judging. If the judge realizes that you are a novice, he may say a few words, in an attempt to calm and relax you. This does not mean that he's inviting you to have a lengthy conversation. It is inappropriate to tell the judge about your dog's show record or any of his previous wins. The judge will not be persuaded if you tell him, "My dog needs only one more win to finish his championship."

Not everyone can win and you must learn to take both the wins and the losses with equal grace. Don't jump wildly about screaming and yelling if you win. Likewise, don't storm out of the ring stamping your feet if you should loose. There will be another show on another day and your dog will have another chance to win. Thank the judge for the ribbon he gives you. If you really feel that the judge did a bad job and doesn't know the breed, then just don't enter your dog at shows where he officiates. Congratulate the winner in a pleasant tone of voice. Dog showing has been called a "gentleman's sport." By acting courteously, you can help keep it that way.

13

The TFT in Obedience

In recent years, the Toy Fox Terrier has made his presence felt in obedience circles. It's high time these little dogs were recognized for their intelligence and trainability. TFT owners are now realizing that obedience training is just as beneficial to a toy dog as it is to a larger breed. Recent outstanding performances by TFTs have done much to dispel the notion that this breed is too "hyper" and energetic to successfully compete in obedience trials. We all know that Toy Fox Terriers are smart. Obedience training gives them the opportunity to prove it.

Let's look at some of the day-to-day, practical applications of training. How many times have you opened your front door, only to have your TFT run out? If your dog knows the "stay" command, he'll remain in place, when the door is opened. This command will also come in handy when you must open your car door. It's also very convenient to have your dog trained to "come" on command. Surely, you've watched someone attempt to chase and corner a TFT. The dog runs wildly about, darting here and there, just out of reach. With growing frustration and rising blood pressure, the owner chases the dog. By the time the dog is finally captured, the TFT is exhausted and the owner is fuming. How much nicer to tell the dog to "come" and have him respond immediately. Should your dog escape from your yard, obedience training might well save his life. If your dog hightails it for the street, a "down" command will cause him to drop immediately. This response might prevent him from ending up under the wheels of a car.

In addition to the practical advantages of owning a trained dog, there are other benefits. Obedience training is an ideal way to form a close bond with your dog. No other activity develops such an intimate rapport between owner and dog. You and your TFT will learn to function as a team. Most Toy Fox Terriers are eager to please and they genuinely enjoy learning. Training also helps to constructively channel this breed's abundant energy. Furthermore, trained dogs are generally happy dogs. They are a pleasure to take out in public and they help to give people a positive impression of the breed.

A BRIEF INTRODUCTION TO TRAINING

Obedience training your dog is not difficult. Dog clubs, in many cities, hold weekly training classes, during which the owner is taught to train his dog.

Jerri Lindsey and U-UD "PR" Adam's Beth, known as Abby, show the proper way to put on a choke collar. (Warren Landry photo)

There are also numerous books which give step-by-step instructions for training. By devoting a few minutes each day to working with your dog, you can have a well-trained companion in short order. Even if you have no desire to participate in obedience competition, your dog will benefit from learning the basic commands. While we cannot include in-depth training instructions here, we will give you an idea of how to teach your dog the basics.

For basic training, your dog will need a suitable collar. A slip (often called a "choke" collar) is best. For Toy Fox Terriers a light weight, small link chain which slides easily, is preferred. It's also possible to purchase a nylon choke collar. It's important that the collar fit properly. When the collar is pulled tight against the dog's neck, there should be about three inches of spare collar. Contrary to its name, the choke collar is not meant to choke a dog. Used properly, it applies quick pressure to the dog's neck and is immediately released. Such collars are not cruel or harmful. You'll also need a leash. A five or six-foot leather or nylon web leash is best. Chain leads are hard on the hands and will telegraph any corrections to the dog.

Every dog should learn the five rudimentary exercises that are the basis for all obedience training. The dog should be able to "sit" on command. He should walk at your side, or "heel," on and off the leash. He should be taught to drop, or "down," when ordered. He should also learn to "stay" when so instructed. Finally, he should "come" when called. We'll

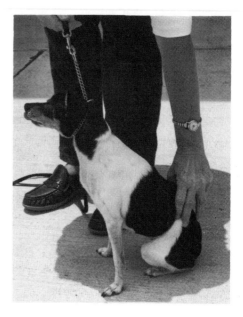

Jerri Lindsey and Abby show how to teach the sit. (Warren Landry photo)

108

describe for you, briefly, the basic methods of teaching each of these five essentials. Regrettably, space allows us to give only the briefest of instructions.

The Sit

To teach the sit, place your dog on a leash. With the dog at your left side, give him the command to "sit." Hold the leash in your right hand. Pull straight up on the leash, while applying downward pressure to the dog's haunches with your left hand. Repeat the command so that the dog associates it with the action. Take your hand away. The dog should remain in a sitting position. Beginning dogs will likely stand up. Don't be annoyed. Place your dog back in a sitting position and tell him, once again, to "sit." When he has remained in place for a few seconds, praise him. Be sure to tell your dog how wonderful he is for obeying you.

The Down

There are two ways to teach the "down" and both are effective. With your dog in a sitting position, give him the hand signal and the command, "down." You can give a small downward jerk with the leash and pull the dog down. Or, with one hand, pull your dog's front legs so they are extended out in front of him. With the other hand, press down on the dog's shoulders. As soon as your dog is down, tell him "down, good." Now, remove your hands from the dog. If he stays where he is, all is well. It's likely, however, that he will sit up again. Repeat the procedure. You may want to pet the dog while repeating, "down, good." If the dog starts to rise while you're stroking him, tell him "no," place your hand on his withers and press down, repeating

Nancy Fishinger and Ch. U-CD "PR" Fishinger's Elvis demonstrate the down. Note the hand signal Nancy uses.

"down, good." This will keep him in place. When your dog stays for a few seconds, praise him.

The Stay

This is one of the most important of the obedience commands and one that will come in handy in everyday life. Have your dog on the leash and place him in a sitting position. Stand in front of your dog. Hold the leash, partially folded, in your left hand. Hold the leash tautly, slightly behind your TFT's head. Give the dog the "stay" signal and the voice command. With the taut leash, you'll be able to keep your dog in place should he try to move. If he doesn't try to get up, take a couple of steps backward and let the leash go slack. The dog may get up and try to follow you. Tell him "no," put him back in position and tell him, again, to "stay." Gradually, you will increase your distance from the dog until you are at the end of the leash. You will also want to lengthen the amount of time you spend away from your dog. The "stay" should be used with both the "sit" and "down" commands. Be sure to praise your dog when he stays successfully.

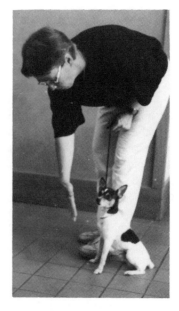

Nancy Fishinger gives Elvis the stay signal before leaving him.

The Recall

Place your dog in the "sit" position. Tell him to "stay." Walk to the end of the leash and call your dog. You'll note that in the other exercises, you have given the dog a single word command. However, since you want the dog to move in this exercise, you'll use his name first. In an excited voice, say, "Spot, come." Keep the tone of your voice light and enthusiastic. Praise the dog as he moves toward you. Most dogs will immediately come to you. Use both hands to reel in the leash, as he comes to you, so that he won't get tangled in it. Tell your dog to "sit" when he is in front of you. If your dog does not respond to the "come" command, give a jerk and reel him to you with the leash. If your dog seems lackadaisical about coming, give the leash

Jerri Lindsey and U-UD "PR" Adam's Beth demonstrate the recall (Warren Landry photo)

110

a quick jerk and, with small steps, run backwards. This usually prompts the dog to run to you. As before, have the dog sit. Your dog has now learned to "come" on command and much praise is due him.

Heeling

There are a few basics to remember when teaching your dog to "heel." The dog is always on the handler's left side. This is referred to as the "heel" position. In heeling, the dog should walk quietly at your left side. His shoulder should be in line with your leg. He should not forge out in front of you, nor should he lag behind. Your dog should be attentive and learn to keep up with any changes in your pace. If you speed up or slow down, the dog should, too. If you make a turn or a turn around, the dog should turn with you.

Place the dog in a sitting position, at your left side. Take a step forward with your left foot. Simultaneously, give a little jerk on the collar and command, "Spot, heel." Remember, this is an active command, in which the dog will be moving. Therefore, use his name first. Start by walking in a straight line or a circle. If the dog starts to forge ahead or move off to the side, give a quick jerk and repeat the command, "Spot, heel." A small jerk, which brings the dog back in position, is all that is necessary. If needed, several successive jerks may be used, but you do not want to drag the dog. You may want to talk to your dog enthusiastically while he's heeling. This will keep the dog's focus on you. Remember, you want the training to be fun, not drudgery. Now, halt. Tell your dog to "sit." Be ready to reach down and help guide the dog into an automatic sit. Anytime you stop, your dog should routinely sit. Keep heeling with your dog, giving small jerks whenever he veers from heel position.

Next, you'll want to teach your dog to do an about turn. When executing an about turn, you want to either pivot or take small mincing steps. You should always reverse your direction by turning to the right. Your TFT may well continue on in the direction he was going when you made your turn. As you begin your turn, give your dog a quick jerk and reiterate the command, "Spot, heel."

Your dog should also be taught to make right and left turns. Your turns should be abrupt and sharp in angle. Right turns are seldom a problem. Simply, give the dog the heel command and a short jerk when beginning your turn. Left hand turns are a little trickier. Since the Toy Fox Terrier is so small, you'll have to take care to avoid stepping on your dog when

Nancy Fishinger and Ch. U-CD "PR" Fishinger's Elvis show the proper position for a dog, when heeling. Note that Elvis' shoulder is in line with Nancy's leg.

you turn. Early in the training, use the lead to let the dog know what is coming up. Take small mincing steps or brush your foot along the ground, when making the turn. If the dog starts to move away, a small jerk will bring him back to position.

Your dog has now learned the basics of heeling. Eventually, you'll want to try heeling off leash with him. Don't be too quick to try your dog off leash, however. Starting him too soon may set back the training. Make sure your dog is working perfectly on lead and paying close attention to you, before you try working off leash.

Unfortunately, the above discussion gives only the briefest possible treatment of the basics. We strongly encourage you to sign up your TFT for obedience classes. If none are available in your area, purchase a book on obedience and start at home. Both you and your Toy Fox Terrier will benefit from the experience.

One final note regarding obedience training. Praise and correction are the basis for all training. Most Toy Fox Terriers are eager to please. You will build on this by giving your dog profuse praise, whenever he does anything right. Always try to be consistent in everything you do. Variations in the way you give commands, or corrections, will confuse your dog and delay the training process. Keep the training light and make it fun. Your voice should radiate enthusiasm and delight. Never, under any circumstances, lose your temper. This can be very difficult to carry out. There will be times when you will become frustrated and angry. You'll be tempted to scream and yell and may want to hit your dog. Don't! Hang up the leash and begin again when you've calmed down. Just don't give up. Patience and consistency are important in all types of training.

OBEDIENCE COMPETITION

The United Kennel Club offers three obedience titles to dogs who demonstrate their proficiency in trials. These are the Companion Dog degree (U-CD), the Companion Dog Excellent title (U-CDX) and the Utility Dog degree (U-UD). A specified series of exercises is required for each competitive level. A perfect score is 200 points, and a dog must earn at least 170 points to qualify for a "leg" toward his degree. Furthermore, the dog must score at least half the points allotted to each exercise to earn a qualifying score. A Toy Fox Terrier must demonstrate his proficiency by earning three legs, in order to qualify for his title. These scores must be awarded under at least two different licensed obedience judges. Jumping is required in each level of U.K.C. obedience competition. Toy Fox Terriers are measured and required to jump the height of their withers. A complete set of the U.K.C.'s obedience regulations are printed annually in *Bloodlines*. You can obtain the regulations by writing to the U.K.C..

We would like to offer a pictorial presentation of the various exercises required in each level of obedience competition. We are fortunate in having two history making dogs to demonstrate these exercises for us. Our special thanks to Nancy L. Fishinger, of Orlando, Florida, owner-trainer of CH. U-CD "PR" Fishinger's Elvis. Elvis is the first male Toy Fox Terrier to earn an obedience title, as well as the first Champion obedience title holder. This little guy certainly demonstrates that beauty and brains do go together. Our deep gratitude to U.K.C. obedience judge, Jerri K. Lindsey, of Ft. Worth, Texas. Jerri is the owner-trainer of the record breaking, U-UD "PR" Adam's Beth. "Abby," as she is known, is the first female obedience title holder and the only Toy Fox Terrier to have earned all three obedience degrees. Abby's not resting on her laurels, though. She and Jerri are now taking lessons in tracking. They hope that, when the U.K.C. adopts a tracking program, Abby will be the first TFT to be awarded her U-TD. Our congratulations to these pioneering owners and their dogs. We only hope that they will be joined shortly by many more TFTs.

THE COMPANION DOG (U-CD) EXERCISES

Ch. U-CD "PR" Fishinger's Elvis on the "Honoring" exercise. The dog is placed in a "Down, Stay," while another dog performs the heeling exercises. (35 points)

Heeling exercises include the "Heel on Leash" and the "Figure 8." Here, Jerri and Abby perform the "Figure 8." (35 points) (Warren Landry photo)

Elvis shows the "Stand for Examination." The dog must stand still, while the judge examines him. This exercise is done off leeash. (30 points)

Elvis performs the "Long Sit." In this group exercise, all dogs are given the "Stay" command and must remain in place for one minute. (30 points)

Nancy and Elvis in the "Heel Off Leash" exercise. Basically the same as the "Heel On Leash," but there is no "Honoring" dog in the ring, and no "Figure 8" is included. (35 points)

Ch. U-CD "PR" Fishinger's Elvis is shown clearing the high jump in the "Recall Over the Jump" exercise. Here we demonstrate the dog's willingness to come to his handler when called, even when obstacles are present. (35 points)

THE COMPANION DOG EXCELLENT (U-CDX) EXERCISES

The "Honoring" exercise is included in the CDX, or "Open," exercises. The dog "Stays" while another competitor performs the "Heel Off Leash" and the Figure 8." (30 points)

The "Heel Off Leash" follows the same pattern as that used in the CD competition. In Open, however, the dog is required to perform the "Figure 8" off leash. (40 points)

Abby, owned by Jerri Lindsey, demonstrates the "Broad Jump." (20 points) (Warren Landry photo)

Ch. U-CD "PR" Fishinger's Elvis showing the dumbbell used in the "Retrieve on the Flat" exercise. The dumbbell is thrown and, on command, the dog must run out and retrieve it, bringing it to his handler. (20 points)

114

Abby shows the "Retrieve Over the High Jump." This exercise is similar to the "Retrieve on the Flat," but the dog must leap the high jump. (30 points) (Warren Landry photo)

Jerri and Abby demonstrate the "Drop On Recall." In this exercise, the dog is left at one end of the ring in a "Stay." The handler then goes to the opposite side of the ring and calls his dog. On a signal from the judge, the handler gives a "Down" signal to his dog. The handler then calls his dog to him. (30 points) (Warren Landry photo)

THE UTILITY DOG (U-UD) EXERCISES

The Utility exercises include the "Signal and Heeling" exercise. In this routine, the dog "Heels," "Stands," "Stays," goes "Down" and "Comes," strictly through the use of hand signals. (40 points)

Jerri Lindsey's U-UD "PR" Adam's Beth demonstrates the "Scent Discrimination" exercise. The dog is asked to determine the article that has been impregated with his handler's scent. He must select this one and bring it to his handler. (30 points) (Warren Landry photo)

Abby, with one of the gloves used in the "Directed 'Marked' Retrieve." In this exercise, three gloves are dropped about the ring. The dog is told which one to pick up and bring to his handler. (20 points) (Warren Landry photo)

115

In the "Directed 'Signal' Retrieve," the dog is instructed to go out and is then commanded to stop, turn around and sit. He then retrieves one of three gloves and returns it to his handler. (30 points)

Utility competition includes the "Consecutive Recall." The dog does a "Drop on Recall" followed by a regular "Recall." (40 points)

One of the great crowd pleasers at obedience trials is the "Directed Jumping" exercise. The dog is instructed to "Go Out" away from his handler. He is then commanded to stop and sit. The handler calls the dog and instructs him to take a jump on the way back. Here we see Abby as she takes both the "Bar Jump" and the "High Jump." (40 points) (Warren Landry photo)

14

The Versatile TFT

In the past, the Toy Fox Terrier has been thought of primarily as a pet and a show dog. In recent years, however, more and more owners have discovered that their little dogs are amazingly versatile. As the breed grows in popularity, we will, no doubt, see Toy Fox Terriers put to even more imaginative uses. In fact, the TFT's abilities seem limitless. While it would be impossible to detail all the myriad services performed by TFTs, we would like to present a few examples. We salute the owners and trainers who daily break new ground for the breed. It is our hope that TFTs will reach ever greater levels of achievement.

TFTS IN SHOW BIZ

As we've seen, in the early 1900's, little Fox Terriers thrilled rural audiences in "dog and pony" shows. Today, Californian Marge Rutherford continues that tradition. Marge owns a unique troupe of toy entertainers. *Canine Capers,* as Marge has dubbed her ensemble, performs at rest homes, schools and homes for handicapped children.

It would be hard to imagine a person more eminently qualified to perform as canine ringmaster. Marge obtained her first purebred dog, an Irish Terrier, in 1938. This was an exciting time in the world of purebred dogs. The American Kennel Club had just launched the sport of dog obedience. Marge says that she learned to train largely by "trial and error." Clearly, Marge learned her lessons well, for she joined the staff of the famous Hollywood Dog Training School. For seven years she worked under the renowned trainer Carl Spitz. Mr. Spitz learned his craft from Germany's illustrious Inspector Schultz, who was responsible for the widespread use of dogs by many European police units. So famous was the "College for Dogs," that the pets of many Hollywood celebrities were enrolled. It was while working for Mr. Spitz that Marge had her first introduction to canine entertainers. She handled the famous Saint Bernard, "Neil," in some of the episodes of the *Topper* television series.

After twenty years of involvement with dogs, Marge Rutherford decided to put together her own crew of four-legged entertainers. She opted for the toy breeds because they were easier to transport. The numerous props necessary for

Marge Rutherford and the equipment used in the steeplechase portion of her *Canine Capers*. (Tom Elder photo)

the performances were also smaller in scale. Marge is impressed with the intelligence and capacity of her little dogs. She says that what they can do is amazing. *Canine Capers* began with several Chihuahuas and a Pomeranian. The dogs play pianos, dance and walk tightropes. Several Toy Fox Terriers have since joined Marge's troupe. The photos clearly demonstrate Marge's success! The "steeplechase" has proven extremely popular. No doubt, Marge Rutherford and her performing TFTs have brightened the day for many people!

HANDI-TFTS

One of the most impressive and unusual uses of the Toy Fox Terrier is as a "Handi-Dog." Judy Guillot, of Tucson, Arizona, is a pioneer of this inventive use of the TFT. Judy, a medical technologist, is confined to a wheelchair. Through the use of her dogs, "PR" Meadowood's Jillian (bred by John Davidson) and her daughter, "PR" Casas Adobe's Amber, Judy's life has been made easier.

The brainchild of founder Alamo Reaves, "Handi-Dogs" was formed, in 1974, to train dogs to aid the handicapped. For the wheelchair bound individual, the Handi-Dog retrieves dropped articles and brings objects, such as shoes and newspapers. The dogs are also trained to bark, in the event a disabled person should fall. In addition, the organization also trains dogs to aid the hearing impaired.

Handi-Dog owners have discovered, however, that the dogs serve more than physical needs. Alamo Reaves speaks of the psychological advantages of

118

a canine assistant. "When you experience a physical crisis, whether it be paralysis, loss of limbs, or crippling illness, you suffer psychologically, too. You tend to lose your sense of worthiness and to wallow in self pity. But a dog loves you even when you don't like yourself, and I find it hard to stay depressed very long with my dogs needing me and telling me in their own way, how wonderful I am."

Handi-Dog owners train their own dogs, under the supervision of a nurse and trained volunteers. Praise and patience are stressed. Dogs begin with basic obedience and graduate to more advanced training. Dogs who complete the entire course are tested, for final certification. If they pass the examination, they become "Certified Handi-Dogs." As such, they are entitled to the same privileges accorded seeing eye dogs and may enter restaurants, work places, planes, etc.

Judy Guillot admits the trainers were somewhat skeptical when she entered "PR" Meadowood's Jillian (better known as Asa) and Amber in the training sessions. Other toy breeds had proven unsuitable. Asa and Amber, however, surprised the skeptics. Even before the training classes were completed, Asa's performance had earned a place for her and Judy on the Handi-Dog demonstration team. On graduation night, in a class of twenty-four dogs, Asa stood proudly in first place among the obedience entrants. The judge awarded Asa, the smallest dog in the class, a near perfect score. She was proclaimed "Best Handi-Dog." Not to be left out, six month old Amber, placed third.

Encouraged by this success, Judy Guillot plans to continue. She hopes Asa and Amber will become the first and second Toy Fox Terrier Certified Handi-Dogs! We hope they'll be the first of many TFTs to help grant a measure

"PR" Hopkins' Loren Ace, one of Marge Rutherford's star performers, takes one of the steeplechase jumps. (Tom Elder photo)

of independence to their disabled owners. (Those wishing to support the work of Handi-Dogs will find the address in the appendix.)

MENTALLY SOUND TFTS

CH. U-CD "PR" Fishinger's Elvis, owned by Nancy L. Fishinger, of Orlando, Florida, made history when he became the first male Toy Fox Terrier to earn an obedience title. Now, Elvis and Nancy have done it again! Elvis is now the first Toy Fox Terrier to have earned a "TT" from the American Temperament Test Society. He now adds the designation, TT-1-TFT to his name.

The American Temperament Test Society was founded in 1977. This national organization serves

PoHo the clown, alias Harry Corty, of New York City, and his talented TFT, Spartan, entertain the crowd. The TFT's intelligence and agility make him an ideal canine entertainer.

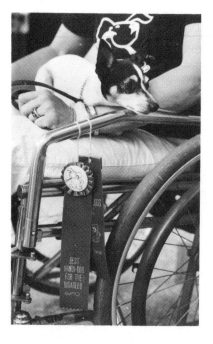

"PR" Meadowood's Jillian takes a well deserved rest in Judy Guillot's lap. (David Ring photo)

breeders by offering tests which demonstrate a dog's inherent genetic temperament. ATTS holds temperament evaluations, in which dogs are exposed to a variety of stimuli. The dog's emotional reaction is evaluated by a panel of three licensed judges, and the dog either passes or fails. Mentally sound dogs must have the ability to distinguish between threatening and non-threatening situations. The tests are designed to weed out inherently shy or overly aggressive dogs.

The ATTS tests simulate situations that the dog might encounter in every day life. The dog and his owner are approached by neutral, friendly and threatening strangers, and the dog's reaction is observed. Reactions to strange noises and sights are also tested. The dog's willingness to walk on strange footing forms another part of the test.

Dogs who pass the ATTS test are issued a certification number. To the best of our knowledge, U-CD "PR" Fishinger's Elvis is the only Toy Fox Terrier to be tested, to date. We should all be proud that this little trailblazer performed so admirably. ATTS testing is one way to ensure that all TFTs will have stable temperaments.

THE HUNTING TFT

While the TFT is indeed a toy breed, he still retains many of the essential terrier characteristics. Lately, many owners are taking to the fields with their little dogs, to prove that they still possess these terrier attributes. Hunting with your Toy Fox Terrier is one of the best ways to assure that the breed's inherent capabilities will remain intact. Owners have also discovered that they can have a great deal of fun, hunting with their TFTs.

Some owners have shied away from hunting their little dogs, because they don't wish to endanger them. However, there are types of hunting in which even the smallest TFT can safely participate. "Mousing" is an ideal sport, in which almost all Toy Fox Terriers can take part. Since mouse hunting does not involve the use of firearms, it is a relatively safe form of field work. Mousing will afford an opportunity for your TFT to demonstrate the attributes of a hunter. For mousing, the dog will need good scenting ability, courage, agility and endurance. These are, after all, the qualities that should be present in every Toy Fox Terrier.

If you have access to a field, you may want to try mousing with your dogs. Even puppies will find delight in this endeavor. If you're using someone

"PR" Meadowood's Jillian in position next to Judy Guillot's wheelchair. (David Ring photo)

Asa and Judy during a competition in Tucson, Arizona. We should all be proud of this very talented duo. (David Ring photo)

else's land, be courteous. Ask for permission to hunt your dogs. Once the property owner discovers that you are after mice, chances are he will be more than happy to oblige. In many parts of the country, mousing can be a year round sport. In the snowy northern parts of the country, summer is best.

Field mice are most commonly found in grassy overgrown fields. You may also want to check in fencerows, as these are common places for the rodents to nest. It may take some practice to spot the mouse's nest, but you'll usually see a cluster of very fine grasses. Take a four or five foot long stick with you and poke the grass. Make sure your dogs are by your side. If you've found a nest, the inhabitants will scurry away when you probe. You'll have to watch your dogs closely or you may not be able to tell that they've gotten anything. Toy Fox Terriers can catch the mouse, kill it and leave it with amazing speed. If you find an empty nest, point it out to your dogs. Even though it's bare, it will still be

TFT fanciers Ernest and Gilbert Young introducing puppies to a racoon. Ernest Young has been one of this country's leading advocates of hunting with Toy Fox Terriers.

122

heavily impregnated with scent. Your dog will often be able to take the scent and follow it until he finds the previous occupants. Encourage him if he does, for he's getting the idea of what hunting (albeit on a small scale) is all about. Most TFTs catch on to mousing quickly, but if your dog proves slower, don't give up. Just keep with it and soon you'll have your very own four-footed mouse catcher.

There are a few rules you should enforce to be sure that your TFT remains safe while hunting. You will most likely be going into the country to hunt. While mice will not be a problem, your TFT could be exposed to other animals. Make sure that he has a rabies shot for his own protection. Also, and most importantly, never allow your dog to hunt on his own. Most TFTs have a surprising amount of natural hunting instinct. Left to their own devices, they are likely to hunt in hazardous places. Your dog may squeeze under tree roots, scamper under a rocky ledge or go down into a small den. He could become trapped there and be unable to extricate himself. You, not knowing where to look, could lose your dog quite easily. Make sure that hunting is done only when you can accompany the dog. With these simple precautions you'll enjoy a day in the field with your TFT.

Ch. "PR" Cody's Eirwin Royal Billy climbs a tree, in search of a squirrel. His owners, W. D. and Dorothy Cody, of Tulsa, Oklahoma, tell us that Billy caught 25 squirrels this year. As Billy clearly demonstrates, a TFT can be an adept hunter and a show dog, too.

APPENDIX

UNITED KENNEL CLUB, INC.
100 E. KILGORE RD.
KALAMAZOO, MI 49001-5598

TOY FOX TERRIER CLUBS

National Toy Fox Terrier Assn.
President
Dr. John F. Davidson
13400 N. Lakewood Dr.
Dunlap, IL 61525

Secretary/Treasurer
B. J. McDonald
2780 Bailey Rd.
Frisco City, AL 36445

Canadian Toy Fox Terrier Assn.
O. C. Rick Bell
R #1
Beaverton, Ontario
Canada L0K 1A0

S-W Ontario Toy Fox Terrier Assn.
Cynthia Wellwood
592 Wallace St.
Wallaceburg, Ontario
Canada N8A 4K7

Appalachian Toy Fox Terrier Club
George C. Hipp
Box 124C
Belpre, OH 45714

Florida Toy Fox Terrier Assn.
Sue Fitzpatrick
P.O. Box 2240
Palm City, FL 34990

Golden West Toy Fox Terrier Assn.
Chuck Borden
1344 Peter Lynn Dr.
San Diego, CA 92154

Heartland Toy Fox Terrier Assn.
Sandra Stamper
16800 E. 3rd North
Independence, MO 64050

Illinois Toy Fox Terrier Assn.
Billie Huggins
R #2, Box 43B
DuQuoin, IL 62832

Kansas-Oklahoma Toy Fox Terrier Assn.
Shirley Thompson
R #2, Box 233
Shiatook, OK 74070

Kentucky Toy Fox Terrier Assn.
Ronald Byrd
R #1, Box 214
Berger, MO 63014

Lone Star Louisiana Toy Fox Terrier Assn.
Ms. Pat Stevens
3803 Synott #1603
Houston, TX 77082

Maryland Toy Fox Terrier Assn.
Jeri Singleton
117 East Bayview Dr.
Annapolis, MD 21403

Michigan Toy Fox Terrier Assn.
Marsha Shively
3815 Yardley Court
Ft. Wayne, IN 46815

New Mexico Toy Fox Terrier Assn.
Ed Sanders
4421 DeSoto Rd.
Hobbs, NM 88240

No. California Toy Fox Terrier Assn.
Kay Chenoweth
21422 Rizzo Ave.
Castro Valley, CA 94546-6224

Northland Toy Fox Terrier Club
Larry Rosenthal
9375 Wellington Lane
Maple Grove, MN 55369

Ohio Toy Fox Terrier Assn.
Bernice McDermitt
17020 Buckland Holden Rd.
Wapakoneta, OH 45895

Pacific Northwest Toy Fox Terrier Club
Bonita Davis
20185 S. Polehn Dr.
Oregon City, OR 97045

Washington State Toy Fox Terrier Club
Thomas C. Morse
1172 N. Cowiche Rd.
Tieton, WA 98947-9612

Wisconsin Toy Fox Terrier Assn.
Dr. Myles J. Notaro
2925 South Tenth St.
Milwaukee, WI 53215

OTHER ORGANIZATIONS

Handi-Dogs, Inc.
P.O. Box 12563
Tucson, AZ 85732